P9-DVV-944

Donatella Cooks

SIMPLE FOOD
MADE GLAMOROUS

DONATELLA ARPAIA
WITH KATHLEEN HACKETT

PHOTOGRAPHS BY ANNA WILLIAMS

RODALE

Mention of specific companies, organizations, or authorities in this
book does not imply endorsement by the author or publisher, nor does
mention of specific companies, organizations, or authorities imply that
they endorse this book, its author, or the publisher.
Internet addresses and telephone numbers given in this book were
accurate at the time it went to press.

© 2010 by Donatella Arpaia
Photographs © 2010 by Anna Williams

All rights reserved. No part of this publication may be reproduced or
transmitted in any form or by any means, electronic or mechanical,
including photocopying, recording, or any other information storage
and retrieval system, without the written permission of the publisher.

Rodale books may be purchased for business or promotional use or for
special sales. For information, please write to:
Special Markets Department, Rodale Inc., 733 Third Avenue, New
York, NY 10017

Printed in the United States of America
Rodale Inc. makes every effort to use acid-free ∞, recycled paper ♺.

Book design by Jan Derevjanik

Library of Congress Cataloging-in-Publication Data
Arpaia, Donatella.
    Donatella cooks : simple food made glamorous / Donatella Arpaia with Kathleen Hackett.
        p.   cm.
    Includes index.
    ISBN-13   978-1-60529-642-5   hardcover
    ISBN-10   1-60529-642-2   hardcover
  1. Cookery, Italian.   2. Cookery, American.   3. Entertaining.   I. Hackett, Kathleen.
II. Title.
    TX723.A643 2010
  641.5973–dc22   2009052583

Distributed to the trade by Macmillan
2   4   6   8   10   9   7   5   3   1   hardcover

To my mom and dad,
who always believed in me.

–Tella Bella

Contents

INTRODUCTION

One of the best parts of running restaurants for the last 10 years is the amazing people I've had the chance to meet—dozens I've come to call friends. Most have enjoyed great success in their careers, navigating such competitive professions as the law, politics, media, art, and finance with ease. So it never fails to surprise me to observe how tentative—even downright fearful—these normally fearless folks can seem when it comes to entertaining at home. One friend, a former model and the brains behind two Internet start-ups, considers a shrimp ring from the corner deli her "secret weapon." Another friend, an event planner, can arrange a party for 1,000 people using only her Blackberry but becomes paralyzed faced with a dinner for eight. My savvy young assistant, whose multitasking skills are unparalleled, goes slack at the sight of a recipe. Even my sister, a lawyer turned stay-at-home mom who grew up eating my mother's authentic Italian food, can't seem to get herself out of her weekly dry meat loaf food rut.

This book is for them—and all of you equally savvy, stylish, busy women and men, who, despite mastering all you attempt, suffer a crippling lack of confidence upon entering the kitchen.

With my father, my mentor in the restaurant business

Of course not everyone is lucky enough to be born into the restaurant world as I was, though it took me a while to realize that it was where I belonged. After law school and 4 miserable months behind a desk at a Midtown Manhattan law firm, I wised up and followed my heart—and the footsteps of my father, who had come to America from Naples, Italy, with nothing and eventually became a well-known restaurateur.

I opened my first restaurant, Bellini, in Manhattan in 1998, basically faking it until I made it. At least that's how it felt. After struggling to put my hard-earned law degree to good use, working in a restaurant felt more like hosting a party every night.

But then again, in my family, I had always been the one who made sure everyone was having a good time. Who knew it was a talent? Drawing from the food I ate throughout my childhood summers in Naples, where my dad grew up, and Puglia, where my mother was born into a family of 10, I created a menu that was essentially an homage to my culinary roots. About 8 months after opening, I found myself standing in the middle of the dining room with Mary J. Blige and Queen Latifah in one corner, Walter Cronkite and his wife in another, then-police commissioner Howard Safir and billionaire (and future New York City mayor) Michael Bloomberg in another and, well, the Italian men in slick suits who tipped very well, ahem, in yet another. I realized that what allowed such a diverse group of high-wattage people to coexist happily in the same room was me. I had the ability to make each one of them feel as if he or she was the only person there. That's when I knew I was going to make it. Nine restaurant launches later, I'm still here—and the pleasure of feeding people great food glamorously in beautiful settings has become my addiction.

I live the quintessential New York City life, rubbing elbows with the culinary elite and a chic clientele, but behind my Dior shades is a soul deeply attached to the lives of my Apulian and Neapolitan relatives. At home, my cooking style is very much indebted to the summers I spent on my grandmother's farm in Toritto in Puglia. There, in the orchards, gardens, and kitchens of my six aunts, my food sensibility was formed. Not a single one of the sisters was what you would call glamorous—think housedress and slippers for a more accurate visual—but they were using the freshest ingredients and preparing them simply, and those are the keys to becoming a good cook no matter who you are (or what you wear).

Presiding over a restaurant every night, however, does have its advantages, particularly when it comes to gleaning the tricks and techniques chefs use to bring drama to the plate and, in my role as hostess, knowing how to walk the fine line between sophistication and snobbery. No one entertains solely to give pleasure to others, though. When I serve a meal that delights my guests, whether at home or in a restaurant, I'm fulfilling a deeper need—one that I suspect every cook shares—for approval, admiration, and awe. I get just as much pleasure out of hosting as my restaurant customers and guests in my home do being there.

In Puglia, and picking olives in my mother's Puglian olive grove

Judging *Iron Chef America*

Learning to make pasta with Zia Rosinella

DONATELLA COOKS

Making orechiette with Zia Rosinella

Before you protest that I have access to better ingredients, teachers, and other resources than you do, let me say unequivocally: You do not have to be an accomplished chef to put a fantastic meal on the table. I know this is a tough concept to wrap your heads around, but once you let go of the idea that you need to reproduce the restaurant meals you order so proficiently, you'll be well on your way to entertaining like a superstar.

Donatella Cooks is a blueprint of my cooking and entertaining strategies. It will help you with everything from shopping for great ingredients to hosting a perfect evening. The recipes that follow are rooted in the dishes of my Southern Italian heritage, with some influences from neighboring Spain and Greece. They also reflect more than a decade of working with great chefs—and stealing their secrets. None ask you to have a mastery of complex techniques, but they all must be made with the freshest, finest ingredients you can find. In fact, the recipes are arranged by season to reinforce the fresh-ingredient rule. The ingredients, in general, are few, which is another reason to seek out the best.

Taste is only part of the culinary equation, though. Customers return to my restaurants again and again, not only because the food is delicious, but also because it's presented beautifully and always with a little drama. We eat with our eyes first, and the easiest way to make it seem like you've spent a lot of time in the kitchen is to arrange food on the plate artfully. And choose those plates carefully. In my house it's the tableware, not chef-y knife skills, that makes the presentation special. I'm not going to ask you to bake your own bread or make your own pasta or pizza dough, and I am not opposed to accompanying dishes with items picked up from the gourmet food shop or specialty purveyors. I encourage you to pull together a spread from fine cheeses and charcuterie, olives, and fresh fruit—all picked up at the store—when the occasion calls for it.

Take it from someone who has been fortunate enough to eat at many of the world's finest restaurants: One of life's great pleasures is cooking—and eating—at home. The benefits are manifold in terms of health, finances, romance, and profession. There's no easier way to make your

Testing family recipes with Kathleen Hackett, Mom, and Zia Donata

fabulous life even more so. It may seem contradictory that as a restaurateur I am extolling the virtues of home cooking, but making your own food rather than reservations has a lot going for it. If you are desperate to shed a few pounds, do the cooking yourself and I guarantee that you'll succeed. If you're a parent, you'll know a lot more about what your kids are eating. And there's no better way to network than to invite colleagues into your home, because all attention will be focused on you. Finally, a new relationship can go from fledgling to full-blown when you bring home-cooked food into the equation. Yes, the way to a man's heart . . . well, you get where this is going.

Just trust me. Let me take you by the hand and soon you will be able to add cooking and entertaining to your long list of talents. So, clear the dining room table of the mail, your laptop, and newspapers, and start cooking. I promise you won't regret it—and you may even fall in love with it.

DONATELLA'S
KITCHEN

The Pantry

I have been accused of being a bit compulsive when it comes to keeping my pantry stocked and orderly. It's partly because I don't get an opportunity to shop regularly and also because I like knowing that I really can whip up something great to eat relying only on what's in my cupboards and in my tiny potted herb garden. The orderly part is a habit that I adopted after watching great chefs at work. The best ones follow the adage "a place for everything and everything in its place"—known in their world as *mise en place*. And, as chefs do in a restaurant kitchen, I transfer ingredients from their original packaging to storage containers—flour, sugar, salt, spices, you name it—and label them with my label maker (which I love), though a piece of masking tape and a permanent marker will do the job nicely, too.

My pantry is full of essentials for cooking the foods I was raised on. You'll always find a few jars of my mother's tomatoes, beans of many kinds, herbs and spices, and, of course, pastas in all shapes. That's the one-foot-in-Puglia side of me. Then there are the nonessential yet critical ingredients I have on hand—the bling, if you will, that brings drama to the table.

Before you add anything to your pantry, though, edit what you already have. Throw out anything other than canned items that has been there for more than 6 months. Dried spices and herbs, in particular, lose their potency much more quickly than you'd imagine. Once you've made some space, designate a shelf for canned goods, one for grains, another for baking ingredients, and so on. Store frequently used items within arm's reach; if you don't bake much, tuck those items away on a higher shelf (seems so obvious, but you'd be surprised). When you're ready to restock, resist the temptation to hit the big box stores. Even if you live in the Taj Mahal with cabinet space to burn, buying in bulk can be wasteful. Are you really going to use a gallon jar of artichoke hearts? Instead, get clicking. Shopping for food online is as easy as buying shoes and handbags there. I use two sites more than any other and highly recommend them:

- **WWW.AMAZON.COM** Who would have thought! The gourmet foods section is literally a one-stop shop for top-quality foods. It seems each time I log on, the selection of quality producers has expanded and they always have the best prices.

- **WWW.IGOURMET.COM** Excellent domestic and international artisan cheeses, meats, wines, and chocolates—what more, really, do you need? Its catalog of foods is enormous, and it offers discounts to customers who sign up for its e-mail newsletters. Customer service is excellent, and you can easily find anything you want on this well-designed and visually appealing Web site.

Here's what's in my pantry:

HERBS, SPICES, AND SEASONINGS

These will make your food sing if they're fresh, fall flat if they're not. Store dried herbs and spices in a cool, dry place in tightly sealed containers. I keep mine in a drawer beneath the counter where I do most of my food preparation.

- **Dried herbs:** basil, bay leaves, oregano, rosemary, sage, tarragon, thyme

- **Spices:** allspice, whole dried chiles (not flakes), cinnamon, clove, nutmeg, saffron threads, smoked paprika, star anise, vanilla bean, whole peppercorns, whole dried chiles (pepperoncini), and red-pepper flakes

EXERCISE YOUR GREEN (MANICURED) THUMB

If your kitchen gets lots of sun, think about growing your own herbs. Begin with the herbs most cooks use regularly: basil, chives, mint, flat-leaf (Italian) parsley, rosemary, sage, and thyme. Not only will you always have fresh herbs at your fingertips, but you can tap into your inner Martha and bundle them for hostess gifts. Dark apartment? Check out the AeroGardens (www.aerogrow. com); they look a little weird but work incredibly well. Red Envelope (www. redenvelope.com) has a supremely stylish herb garden kit, and I've also had success with those from www.herbkits. com.

IN THE CUPBOARD

- Canned cannellini beans and chickpeas

- Dried pastas (De Cecco for everyday, Setaro for entertaining) in a variety of shapes including angel hair, bucatini, orecchiette, spaghettini, fusilli, elbows, cavatelli

- Fregola and/or Israeli couscous

- Instant polenta

- Quinoa

- Carnaroli and arborio rice

- Panko bread crumbs

- Dried porcini mushrooms

- Anchovy paste in a tube or jar

- Capers packed in brine

- Slivered almonds; pine nuts; pistachios

- Canned San Marzano tomatoes (whole and crushed)

- Roasted peppers packed in oil

- Sun-dried tomatoes packed in olive oil

- Variety of olive tapenades

- Bella Cucina artichoke pesto

- Several kinds of gourmet crackers and flatbreads (no Stoned Wheat Thins or Ritz, please)

On the baking shelf:

- In addition to the obvious flour, white and brown sugars, and baking soda and powder, I stock confectioners' sugar, powdered unflavored gelatin in packets, pure vanilla extract, orange blossom water, and Nutella

In another cupboard, not too far from the stove but not right next to it either:

- One special extra-virgin olive oil, a less pricey extra-virgin for everyday use, truffle oil (look for an estate-bottled oil stamped with a date), lemon olive oil (fresh lemons are pressed with the olives), and vegetable oil

- Balsamic vinegars (young and a pricey aged one for special occasions); red and white wine vinegars; vincotto (sweet grapes slow-cooked to a syrup); vermouth; Marsala, and red and white wines for cooking

IN THE REFRIGERATOR AND FREEZER

- Parmigiano-Reggiano and pecorino cheese

- Kalamata olives

- Eggs

- Unsalted butter

- Charcuterie (chorizo, hard salami)

- Lemons

- Fresh herbs (see opposite)

- Sparkling water; sparkling wine

- Gourmet ice creams

- Garlic (no cheating with the peeled cloves in a jar)

- Onions

- Small red potatoes

CULINARY "BLING"

Use these specialty ingredients as often as possible:

- Valrhona bittersweet chocolate

- Edible gold leaf and dust

- Pastry rocks (aka Poprocks)

- Sorbets and ice creams in both traditional and exotic flavors (think fior di latte, coffee, pistachio)

- Amaretti di Saronno cookies

- Colored sanding sugars; edible glitter

- Hawaiian sea salt (alea) and other specialty salts (go for varied colors)

- Limoncello or other liqueur decanted into small bottles for hostess gifts

Tools and Equipment

When I observe a chef cooking in the restaurant for the first time, one of the things I immediately note is whether he or she is organized—pots and pans in the right place, proper utensils on hand, streamlined use of gadgets and appliances. Organization is one of the keys to an efficient kitchen and to turning out hundreds of meals every evening without a lot of stress. At home, I hold myself to the same standards, which invariably pays off when I'm cooking for friends and trying to be glamorous at the same time.

Figuring out what tools you really need to feel like a pro in the kitchen is a lot like taking stock of your closet. So it makes sense to approach the cupboards, cabinets, drawers, and counters as you would the racks, boxes, and shelves in your closet. Clear out the clutter, organize the essentials smartly, and limit gadgets and small appliances to those you really use (or *will* use once you have read this book). That means ditching—or better yet, giving to Goodwill—the warped pans, the scratched nonstick skillets, and most of your plastic utensils. Buy a few quality items rather than loading up on a lot of tools, appliances, kits, and sets. You can do without 99 percent of the tools out there to prepare the recipes in this book. One top-quality chef's knife, for example, is far more useful than a boxed set of knives, many of which you will rarely, if ever, use. When you pare down your kitchen wardrobe to the right pieces, it's far easier to cook there.

Your pots and pans have to fit you. In other words, you have to feel comfortable holding the pan by the handle, be strong enough to lift it, and just feel good using it. There are a few crucial features, though. The heavier the pot, the better; thinner gauges warp and dent and transfer heat unevenly. Buy your pots and pans with lids and handles that are sturdy and heatproof (this includes the handle on the lid, too). Avoid glass lids; they're generally not ovenproof and are easy to break. Copper pots and pans, though stunning, are a nightmare to maintain. Truthfully, when I see pristine copper pots and pans in a kitchen, I'm convinced there's not much cooking going on! The one copper item I do own is a bowl for whipping egg whites, which is not a necessity, but it does help to fluff them up faster than a glass or metal bowl. It's a beautiful object, too.

Here are the rock bottom basics:

- **One 8-quart stockpot with lid.** It should be made of a nonreactive material, such as stainless steel or enameled cast iron. Simmer soups in it or make a big batch of ragù, not to mention boiling pasta and steaming vegetables. My Zia Donata mixes up her cheesecake (see page 214) in hers. I prefer Calphalon's (www.calphalon.com) stainless steel stockpot with aluminum core.

- **One 3- to 4-quart sauté pan and one 1- to 2-quart saucepan with lids** are essential. All-Clad (www.all-clad.com) makes stainless steel pans with aluminum sandwiched all the way through that are responsive and durable and go from stove to oven.

- **Large, medium, and small commercial nonstick skillets** can be found at restaurant supply stores. The heavyweight nonstick versions stand up to high heat and restaurant-level wear. The small size will come in handy when you're cooking for yourself. Those by Circulon (www.circulon.com) are durable and reasonably priced.

- **One small (9" x 13") and one large (14" x 16") roasting pan** are indispensable. The smaller one should fulfill most of your needs unless you're tapped to roast the turkey for Thanksgiving, in which case the larger one is a must. I love my All-Clad roasting pans. They're made from heavy-gauge stainless steel, have a nonstick finish (can you say easy cleanup?), and have riveted handles that are roomy enough to accommodate mitted hands. Handles are mandatory—unless you want to burn your fingers off or drop the pan on the floor (been there, done that; not fun).

- **Baking dishes with straight sides**—skip the glass version and go for a more oven-to-table-friendly style of handcrafted clay or colorful enameled cast iron. Staub's (www.staubusa.com) oval stackable dishes are pricey but worth it because you'll never need to replace them, and Le Creuset (www.lecreuset.com) makes my hands-down favorite.

- **Rimmed heavyweight sheet pans** are among the most versatile pans in the kitchen—restaurant kitchens are stacked to the ceiling with them. Buy them in both full and half sheets at restaurant supply stores. The full-size pans may be too big for your oven so measure before buying.

- **A cast-iron stovetop grill pan** is ideal for those, like me, who live in apartments with no outdoor space for grilling. I have used a classic cast iron pan in the past, which most closely approximates the char of an outdoor grill, but the truth is it takes work to maintain cast iron. Now I use Le Creuset's (www.lecreuset.com) nonstick enameled cast-iron stovetop pan—it does the job nicely and is far easier to clean and maintain.

- **A Dutch oven,** which is essentially a lidded casserole, is great for long, slow simmers and stove-to-oven roasts and stews. I have long used Le Crueset's (www.lecreuset.com) 8-quart enameled cast iron version. These are available in gorgeous colors, and go from oven or stovetop to table beautifully.

KNIVES

Finding the right knife is a lot like finding the right guy: You'll have to try a few to find your perfect match, but with enough TLC it should last you a lifetime. While dozens are available for purchase online, I strongly suggest you hold one in your hand before handing over your credit card. I prefer Wüsthof brand knives because they're a great fit for me. Never put knives in the dishwasher—it dulls the blades. Electric sharpeners do, too. I have my knives sharpened every couple of months by a local professional. Look online to find out where you can bring them in your area. Always rinse and dry knives promptly after each use and store them on a mounted magnetic strip or side by side in a padded drawer.

Ultimately, you really only need three knives:

- **An 8" chef's knife** made of forged steel

- **A paring knife** (3" to 4" long) for peeling fruit and vegetables, coring tomatoes, and such

- **A 9" or longer serrated bread knife**

SMALL APPLIANCES

There are truly only four small appliances that you need to make fabulous food:

- If you don't already own an **immersion blender**, buying one will change your life—or at least the way you make creamy soups. What's more, it takes up almost no room in the cabinet. There are two kinds: One features a fixed blade, and the other comes with attachments including a whisk. I prefer the multitasking version with the attachments.

- **A mini food processor** and a **2-quart food processor** make fast work of serious mixing jobs, the former ideal for small-quantity sauces and the latter indispensable for making doughs in minutes.

- Lastly, there's not a single recipe in the following pages that requires a stand mixer—**a hand mixer** will do just fine. Buy one with multiple attachments to stretch its usefulness.

SMALL TOOLS

It's the little things that count, or at least that's the case in a well-stocked kitchen. The right small tools are like perfect accessories; they help you pull a meal together with seeming ease. Using the right tool for the right job ratchets up your cooking cred, especially if you're performing in front of guests. There's a mind-boggling array of kitchen gadgets out there. Stick to this list and skip the rest.

- **Tongs (12" and 16" long)**

- **Kitchen scissors**

- **Spatulas** in various sizes and materials (offset stainless steel, heat-resistant nylon for nonstick pans, and silicone, not rubber, which is not heat-resistant or dishwasher safe)

- **Slotted spoon**

- **Wooden spoon** (essential for making risotto)

- **Ladle**

- **Spider** (for transferring pasta from the pasta water to the pan with the sauce)

- **Balloon and standard wire whisks**

- **Colander**

- **Several plastic cutting boards**

- **Sturdy box grater**

- **Lightweight, heatproof stainless steel nesting mixing bowls** (check restaurant supply stores for these)

- **Stainless steel strainer set**

- **Dry and liquid measuring cups and measuring spoons**

- **Comfortable vegetable peeler**

- **Microplane zester**

- **Pepper grinder**

- **Transparent plastic squeeze bottles** (see Chef Tip)

chef tip

One of the secrets behind every chef's beautiful plating technique is a 99-cent plastic bottle with a conical tip, much like the ketchup dispensers at a hot-dog stand. These squeeze bottles are like paintbrushes—chefs use them to drizzle finishing sauces, thin purees, and dressings artfully onto plates before they make their way to the table. Throughout this book, you will notice I say to drizzle sauces and liquid garnishes onto the plate. You can certainly do this straight from the bowl (using a spoon, in that case), but if you want to up the presentation ante, use a squeeze bottle for greater control—and a chef-worthy result. Squeeze bottles are also great for storing salad dressings.

chapter one HORS D'OEUVRES

Winter

Pecorino Fonduta with Lavender Honey
Bagna Cauda
Baked Buffalo Ricotta
Mixed Italian Salumi with Artisanal Jams
Sautéed Spicy Cracked Olives
Donatella's Popcorn

Spring

Baked Figs with Prosciutto and Gorgonzola
Salmon and Caviar Crostini
Sicilian Tuna and White Bean Bruschetta
Simple Crostini
Bresaola Purses

Summer

Farinata with Fontina and Rosemary
Grilled Swordfish and Watermelon Skewers
Mini Caprese
Seafood Salad in Radicchio Cups

Fall

Zucchini alla Scapece
Greek Pizzettes
Pear and Cinnamon Compote with a Selection of Cheeses
Gorgonzola Dolce, Bacon, and Onion Crostini

Any great dish can be miniaturized. That's probably the most important thing I learned when I was first faced with serving hors d'oeuvres. Even though I was in the restaurant business, the idea of creating the kind of passed canapés that are made by cooks with serious knife skills was daunting. So, at first I turned to the same tried, true, and tired cocktail party solutions—though let the record reflect I never, ever went as far as that horribly mealy shrimp ring that seems to be everywhere. As I began to work closely with chefs, I had a culinary epiphany: It wasn't the ingredients that made a dish an hors d'oeuvre; it was the size. I could miniaturize just about any of the dishes I loved: arugula rolled in a salty strip of bresaola, swordfish steak cut into chunks and threaded onto a little skewer with fruit and cheese, a shot glass or teacup of soup, or risotto served in Asian soup spoons. With a little creativity, nearly any dish can be turned into an hors d'oeuvre.

There *are* a few rules, though. Technically, an hors d'oeuvre shouldn't require a fork or plate and it shouldn't take more than two bites to eat. I'm all for improvising, but these are important points to keep in mind. I know you know what it's like to try to balance a small plate and a drink while engaging in riveting conversation—not fun. Or elegant. I also strongly suggest that you refrain from offering any seriously DIY dishes. Anything that requires more assembly than spreading some dip or placing a piece of cheese on a cracker falls into this category. After all, you're not hosting craft night. As a corollary, avoid leaky, bulky, or otherwise cumbersome hors d'oeuvres that might wind up on a guest's dress or tie.

As for premade items, I once read that Julia Child regularly served Pepperidge Farm goldfish crackers at cocktail hour. That's confidence. You, too, can serve cheese crackers to your guests—once you've thoroughly mastered French culinary techniques as she did! Until then, you'll need to do more than open a package of snacks and dump them into a bowl. I don't mean that you can't open a few containers and boxes of top-quality ingredients and assemble them artfully. In fact, I highly recommend it! If you can count the number of cocktail parties you've hosted on one hand, then 80 percent of your menu *should* consist of recipes you assemble. If you're chronically time-strapped, that's another perfectly valid reason.

Pulling together a spread of hors d'oeuvres with as little actual cooking as possible is really the way to go if you're a novice—or nervous—hostess, because you need to focus on the rest of the meal. Spooning a partially prepared seafood salad (for which you make the dressing) into a radicchio cup or baking fresh ricotta in a foil packet can make you look like a genius in the kitchen. If you do use premade items for your hors d'oeuvre spread, don't broadcast the fact that it didn't come from your kitchen! Replate or decant every single thing onto a platter or into a container. I have a set of beautiful little wooden bowls with matching wooden spoons that I scoop purchased spreads and pestos into. With a quick drizzle of beautiful olive oil and a basket of sliced walnut bread, it appears to have come from my own kitchen. This isn't about taking credit for other people's work, but about making what you serve seem special and in keeping with the style that you want to convey.

There are two characteristics that separate really good hors d'oeuvres from the bad and the ugly: size and packaging. You can make the most delicious hors d'oeuvres in the history of cocktail parties, but if they're thoughtlessly presented—wrong

donatella do's

1 • Dress up a cheese platter with an artisanal honey—chestnut, lavender, or acacia, for example—for instant culinary credibility. Serve it with a honey spool or, if it comes on the comb, set it directly on the serving tray with a small knife for spreading.

2 • Indulge in a proper shrimp cocktail. Put peeled, poached shrimp in a huge bowl filled with crushed ice and lots of lemon wedges. Buy cocktail sauce (usually the fishmonger sells a nice one) and grate fresh horseradish into it to suggest it was homemade.

3 • Smoked fish is a no-brainer hors d'oeuvre. Skip the expected smoked salmon, and try smoked sturgeon or trout.

4 • Always taste purchased spreads—such as artichoke, sun-dried tomato, and olive—before serving them to guests. There are hundreds of brands to choose from, some far superior in taste and quality than others. My favorites are Bella Cucina for the artichoke spread and Colavita for tapenades.

5 • Use paper cocktail napkins if you're serving a crowd; for any fewer than eight, use linen.

6 • Empty the garbage before everyone arrives. You don't want to be dragging it out in front of guests!

7 • Help your guests to be as elegant as you are: If toothpicks or pits are involved, provide an obvious vessel in which to dispose of them. No one wants to spend the night with a fistful of napkins and pits! I set out small bowls and rattan baskets in various spots around the room for discreet disposal.

vessel or worse, wrong size vessel—there goes your entertaining cred. A basic rule of thumb: Go for a look of plenty without overcrowding. Putting 2 cups of olives in a 4-cup bowl makes them look skimpy; piling them in a 1½-cup bowl gives an impression of abundance. Pull together a decent collection of platters, bowls, plates, trays, and serving utensils in varying sizes, then supplement with unusual pieces. Restaurant supply stores (check out www.jbprince.com) are my go-to source for mini cast iron skillets, ramekins in every size, stands for holding paper cones (that you can fill with my over-the-top popcorn, page 14), and so much else. In fact, when I'm navigating the offerings online, I relent on my "no plastic utensils" rule a bit because some of the mini plastic items are adorable. Bamboo items are also plentiful; among my favorites are skewers (no more toothpicks!) and tongs (so cute). Asian soup spoons are another fabulous vehicle for holding pasta, risotta, etc. . . . Hit the bath, office, and storage departments at IKEA for unusual serving pieces, and don't snub other mass retailers such as Crate&Barrel (great for plain white tableware), Pottery Barn (for an occasional decorative table accent) and The Container Store (for an excellent selection of serving vessels). Florist shops and even the hardware store (think slabs of glass, pieces of slate, ceramic tiles to use as platters) are also great places to stock up.

I often find an evening-long cocktail party is the most modern way to entertain. It's partly a reflection of the small-plate trend on restaurant menus and also a matter of practicality: Many who are new to entertaining don't have the gear or the real estate to seat more than eight people comfortably. For an evening-long cocktail party, a mix of light and substantial hors d'oeuvres is a must, as is a tantalizing spread of hors d'oeuvre–size desserts from your favorite patisserie. All of the same presentation rules apply—I have several glass slabs from Pottery Barn that I top with small cookies, chocolates, candies, and gourmet marshmallows. If the savories hadn't already won over your guests, this sweet gesture will make you look like a fabulous host.

Pecorino Fonduta with Lavender Honey

This dish is my answer to baked brie and it's soooo easy to make! At home, I put this on the menu when my guest list includes people who don't know each other. It makes a great conversation starter because this appetizer is one you share.

In my mother's day, a woman had to know how to make a perfect fonduta before her potential mother-in-law would agree to let her son marry. The trick is knowing when to remove it from the heat. There's no guesswork here. Just be sure to ask the cheese seller for a young pecorino; if it's more than 3 years old, it won't melt properly. (See photo page 1.)

SERVES 4 TO 6

YOU'LL NEED:
ovenproof dish
tongs

---

8 ounces young pecorino cheese (aged no more than 3 years), cut into small dice

3 tablespoons hazelnuts, toasted (page 49) and chopped

1 teaspoon red-pepper flakes

1 teaspoon fresh thyme leaves plus a few sprigs for garnish

12 slices rustic Italian bread

1 teaspoon lavender or other artisanal honey

Kosher salt and fresh cracked black pepper

PREHEAT THE OVEN to 350°F.

COMBINE THE CHEESE, nuts, red-pepper flakes, and thyme leaves in a large bowl. Transfer to a 2-cup ovenproof dish and bake until the fonduta is golden brown on the top and the cheese is fully melted.

MEANWHILE, USING TONGS, "grill" the bread slices on both sides over a gas flame or by placing the bread directly on the coils of an electric burner, taking care not to let them char.

PLACE THE WARM CHEESE DISH on a cutting board, drizzle with the honey, season with the salt and pepper, and garnish with the thyme sprigs. Surround with the grilled bread and serve.

Bagna Cauda

Everyone loves this dip—it's chic and understated. And don't be afraid of anchovies; they mellow in the hot oil and butter and make the dish. It's as elegant as a dip gets (far preferable to leaden mayo- or sour cream–based versions) and ridiculously easy to make. For the vegetables, avoid any precut ones. They might save you time, but they're more expensive and less fresh. Check out your farmer's market for unusual vegetable varieties. And rather than piling the vegetables on a large platter, I arrange them in low cylindrical glass vases from the florist or beautiful little bowls. It's a simple way to add a touch of glamour.

SERVES 4 TO 6

YOU'LL NEED:
butter warmer

1 cup extra-virgin olive oil

¼ cup (½ stick) unsalted butter

6 garlic cloves, finely chopped

1 tablespoon anchovy paste or 3 anchovy fillets

3 tablespoons fresh lemon juice

Kosher salt and freshly ground black pepper

3 pounds fresh veggies (such as radishes, fennel chunks, endive spears, and real baby carrots)

MELT THE OLIVE OIL AND BUTTER in a small saucepan over medium heat.

ADD THE GARLIC and cook for 2 minutes, or until softened. Add the anchovy paste, reduce the heat to low, and cook for 5 minutes (using a fork to mash the anchovy fillets, if using, into a paste). Add the lemon juice and salt and pepper to taste and cook a few minutes more. Pour into an earthenware pot or flameproof casserole. Set the pot over a butter warmer or tea candle to keep warm.

ARRANGE THE VEGETABLES in individual containers set on a tray around the bagna cauda and serve.

donatella clicks

I like my butter warmers more than almost anything in my kitchen. Having one on hand is perfect for keeping the bagna cauda warm throughout the cocktail hour. They're great for fondue, chocolate dipping sauce, or any warm dessert sauce. The online catalog www.homegoods.com sells perfect white ceramic butter warmers. It also sells hundreds of things you absolutely don't need but will want.

Baked Buffalo Ricotta

If you're not already BFFs with the guy or girl behind the cheese counter, this dish should be the start of a lifelong friendship. I say this because it's essential that you use high-quality *fresh* ricotta (preferably buffalo ricotta; if you can't get it, go for sheep's milk ricotta)—not the kind you get in a tub at the supermarket. It's the principal ingredient in this dish, so it has to be the best.

I first tasted buffalo ricotta in Naples, my father's birthplace, on a visit to Rita De Rosa, a well-known Neapolitan cook. I loved that she baked the ricotta in humble foil—and each time she made it she put different ingredients in the packet. Tomatoes, olives, fresh oregano, basil—whatever she had on hand was fair game. To this day, I make it in foil and serve it that way, too, to raves.

SERVES 4 TO 6

Extra-virgin olive oil

8 ounces fresh buffalo or sheep's milk ricotta

4–5 cherry tomatoes, halved lengthwise

Fresh oregano leaves

Fleur de sel and freshly ground black pepper

8–12 slices rustic Italian bread

PREHEAT THE OVEN TO 450°F.

DRIZZLE A BIT OF OLIVE OIL onto the center of an 8" x 11" sheet of foil and spread it all over with your fingers. Spoon the ricotta onto the center, spreading it into a small square. Arrange the cherry tomatoes on top, followed by the oregano. Season with the salt and pepper. Oil a second 8" x 11" sheet of foil and place over the ricotta. Fold the foil into a packet, leaving about a ¼" border around the cheese. Remember, you'll be serving directly from the packet, so neatness counts. Place on a baking sheet and bake for 15 to 20 minutes, until piping hot throughout.

MEANWHILE, USING TONGS, "grill" the bread slices on both sides over a gas flame or by placing the bread directly on the coils of an electric burner, taking care not to let them char.

TO SERVE, USE THE TIP OF A KNIFE to cut an "X" into the top of the packet and fold back the points to reveal the cheese. Place on a wooden cutting board and serve with the grilled bread.

donatella clicks

If your cheesemonger or Italian specialty shop doesn't carry fresh ricotta, beg him to begin, or order it online at www.buonitalia.com.

Mixed Italian Salumi with Artisanal Jams

Salumi is a general term for Italian cured meats, primarily pork, but occasionally made with beef as well. Buy the best-quality salumi available and present it beautifully (I prefer a cool slab of rough-edged marble to the ubiquitous rustic cutting board), keeping in mind balance, proportions, and flavors. Three to five varieties will do—at least one each of sweet, hot, and mild salumi. I always include prosciutto, since it's universally beloved, but rather than go for the expected prosciutto di Parma, I prefer the more delicate prosciutto di San Daniele. Decant the jams in pretty little bowls with serving spoons and, if anyone is bold enough to ask, say that you made them.

SERVES 4 TO 6

4 ounces each finocchiona, sopressata, and/or chorizo

3-4 ounces prosciutto, Mortadella, coppa, Serrano, and/or bresaola

2 or 3 assorted flavors artisanal jams and/or chutneys

ARRANGE THE SAUSAGES on a large slab of marble or a decorative cutting board and cut a few thin slices, on the diagonal, from each one. Place a small sharp knife next to each. Intersperse the small bowls of jam among the sausages, each with a demitasse or small serving spoon, and serve.

Sautéed Spicy Cracked Olives

If you've ever fantasized about being able to say, "Sure, come on over. I'll throw a little something together," but don't have the confidence to pull off a spur-of-the-moment dinner, these olives are a good place to start. Why bother with an olive recipe when you can buy a beautiful assortment at the local gourmet food shop? It's like the difference between eating bread warm or at room temperature. Sauté olives in a bit of hot oil, add a few seasonings, and you come out of the kitchen not only looking like a cook, but reminding your friends that you really don't serve everything straight from cans and delivery containers. Cracked olives are nothing more than olives that have been slit or gently bruised before curing so that they absorb the oil (or in some cases, brine) quickly.

I love to pair these with Baked Buffalo Ricotta (page 11), especially if dinner is to follow or if I'm having friends over before a night on the town.

SERVES 4 TO 6

¼ cup extra-virgin olive oil

8 garlic cloves, minced

1½ teaspoons red-pepper flakes

2 cups black cracked olives, packed in olive oil

¾ cup red wine vinegar

Fresh thyme sprig for garnish

HEAT THE OLIVE OIL IN A LARGE SKILLET OVER MEDIUM HEAT. Add the garlic and red-pepper flakes and cook until the garlic is fragrant and soft, about 1 minute. Add the olives and sauté, stirring occasionally, for 3 minutes. Add the vinegar and cook for 8 to 10 minutes, until it has evaporated.

TRANSFER THE OLIVES TO A SMALL SERVING BOWL, garnish with the thyme sprig, and serve. (Remember to tell your guests there are pits!)

chef tip: olive etiquette

One of my biggest party pet peeves is the olive bowl aftermath. If you've ever walked around a party clutching a napkin full of pits and toothpicks, you know what I'm talking about. I'm a stickler for serving olives on the pit (otherwise they tend to be mushy) and just as serious about providing an obvious place to discard those pits. If you don't want to be the pit police, set out a small, cute bowl near the olives—and put a few pits in it as a guide.

Donatella's Popcorn

A smart cook can dress anything up, including popcorn. A humble bowl of salty, buttery popcorn is one thing (mouthwatering, let's face it), but toss it with truffle oil, rosemary, and a little pecorino and it's something else altogether. You're not going to serve it before a formal sit-down (unless you dust it with edible gold, see page 116), but it does lend a bit of elegance to movie night with the girls, a quiet night home with your man, or a holiday cocktail party. Depending on the occasion, serve it in a big wooden bowl, bamboo or paper cones, or sleek cylindrical glass vases. Oh, and never, ever microwave it.

SERVES 6 TO 8

3 tablespoons unsalted butter, melted

2 tablespoons black or white truffle oil

¾ teaspoon kosher salt

Freshly ground black pepper

3 tablespoons vegetable oil

2 tablespoons fresh rosemary

1¼ cups popcorn kernels

½ cup grated imported Pecorino Romano, Parmigiano-Reggiano, or Grana Padano

COMBINE THE BUTTER, truffle oil, salt, and plenty of pepper in a large metal bowl. Set aside.

WARM THE VEGETABLE OIL in a large, heavy pot over medium heat. Add the rosemary and cook for 1 minute to infuse the oil with the herb. Do not let the rosemary burn. Remove the rosemary from the oil using a slotted spoon, and add it to the butter mixture. Add the popcorn to the pot, cover, and stand close by until the corn starts popping. Shake the pan back and forth until the popping has slowed but not stopped entirely. Dump the popcorn into the metal bowl with the butter mixture and immediately toss well to distribute the flavorings evenly. Sprinkle with the cheese, toss again, and transfer to a serving bowl. Serve warm.

Baked Figs with Prosciutto and Gorgonzola

The only way you make a fresh fig more succulent than it already is, is to stuff it with cheese and wrap it in a little pork. Very little can go wrong if the figs are plump and juicy (if they're shriveled, walk on by)—but be sure to wrap the prosciutto just 1½ times around each one. Any more than that and they'll be heavy and messy and no longer fabulous.

Time the baking of these so that they come out of the oven a few minutes after guests arrive. Just assemble them ahead and put in the oven 10 minutes before you want to serve. As a first course, plate 2 stuffed figs and drizzle the balsamic vinegar around them using a squeeze bottle. Garnish with a bit of crumbled Gorgonzola and toasted, chopped pecans (page 49).

SERVES 4 TO 6

¼ cup extra-virgin olive oil, plus extra for coating the pan

12 fresh black Mission figs

6 ounces Gorgonzola

6 slices prosciutto, halved lengthwise, trimmed of most excess fat

Salt and freshly ground black pepper

¼ cup aged balsamic vinegar (at least 5 years)

PREHEAT THE OVEN to 350°F. Coat a baking sheet with olive oil. Make a shallow "X" with a sharp knife into the body of each fig.

ROLL THE GORGONZOLA into 12 small balls and gently press 1 into each fig. Wrap a slice of prosciutto around each fig 1½ times, covering the cheese and leaving the top of the fig exposed. Trim away the excess prosciutto. (If there are too many layers of it, the fig won't crisp up.) Arrange the figs, stem end up, on the baking sheet. Drizzle with the olive oil and season with salt and pepper. Bake until the prosciutto is crisp, about 15 minutes.

ARRANGE ON A PLATTER and drizzle with the balsamic vinegar.

Salmon and Caviar Crostini

You need to know how to make at least one salmon hors d'oeuvre. I know, I know, salmon sounds like a bore, but there's a reason it's a restaurant menu constant. Aside from vegans, nearly *everyone* likes it—picky eaters, kids, grandparents, your mother-in-law. If the occasion calls for less bling, skip the caviar and garnish it with dill. I prefer the subtler flavor of cured salmon (also known as gravlax) to the more assertive smoked variety, but either is fine here. Have your fishmonger cut it into thin slices. I serve these on black ceramic tiles for added drama!

MAKES 12
CROSTINI,
SERVES 4 TO 6

1 cup peeled and small diced seedless cucumber

2 tablespoons distilled white vinegar

2 tablespoons extra-virgin olive oil

½ teaspoon kosher salt

½ teaspoon freshly ground black pepper

8 ounces crème fraîche

1 teaspoon chopped chives

1 teaspoon chopped dill, plus more for garnish

Grated zest of 2 lemons, plus more for garnish

Simple Crostini (page 22)

½ pound best-quality cured salmon (gravlax), plain or dilled

50 grams trout roe or salmon caviar (optional)

TOSS THE CUCUMBER, vinegar, olive oil, and ¼ teaspoon each of the salt and pepper together in a small bowl and set aside at room temperature for 30 minutes. Strain off the liquid. Combine the cucumber, crème fraîche, chives, dill, lemon zest, and remaining ¼ teaspoon of salt and pepper in a small bowl and stir to combine. Cover and refrigerate at least 1 hour.

ARRANGE THE CROSTINI on a serving platter. Top each with a slice of salmon, then top with a dollop of the cucumber mixture. Using a demitasse spoon, dot each with the trout roe or salmon caviar, if using. Garnish with dill and lemon zest and serve.

donatella clicks

Russ & Daughters, home to New York City's best smoked and cured fish, has been around for 100 years. It's as crucial a contact as your hairstylist. If you can't get there, order it online (www.russanddaughters.com).

Sicilian Tuna and White Bean Bruschetta

In Italy, tuna doesn't have to be raw to be sexy. The jarred kind, packed in olive oil, is tossed with everything from pasta to greens to my favorite—cannellini beans. I have these two ingredients in my cupboard at all times, because I'm addicted to the combination. And it's my go-to dish when I have no time to shop!

SERVES 4 TO 6

½ cup extra-virgin olive oil plus extra for brushing

1½ tablespoons red wine vinegar

¼ teaspoon Dijon mustard

1 small garlic clove, minced

½ cup thinly sliced red onion, soaked for 30 minutes in ice-cold water

Kosher salt and freshly ground black pepper

1 (15-ounce) can cannellini beans, rinsed and drained well

1 (250-gram) jar imported olive oil-packed Italian tuna confit, drained

20 fresh mint leaves, cut in thin strips

4–6 slices rustic Italian bread

WHISK TOGETHER ¼ CUP of the olive oil, vinegar, mustard, and garlic in a small bowl. Add half of the onion, toss, and let stand for 5 minutes. Season with salt and pepper.

COMBINE THE BEANS and the onion vinaigrette in a large bowl. Puree one-third of the mixture in a mini food processor until smooth. Fold this mixture back into the beans, add the tuna and the remaining ¼ cup of olive oil, then stir in all but 1 tablespoon of the mint. Mix until the tuna is no longer chunky.

USING TONGS, "grill" the bread slices on both sides over a gas flame or by placing the bread directly on the coils of an electric burner, taking care not to let it char. Cut each in half.

ARRANGE THE BREAD SLICES on a platter. Spoon some of the tuna-bean mixture onto each slice. Garnish with the remaining onions and mint and serve.

donatella clicks

It's not likely to be shelved next to the canned tuna at the grocery store, but Italian tuna confit is available at gourmet and specialty food stores and some supermarkets. If you can't find it, buy it at www.tonninotuna.com.

chef tip

When you open the tuna confit, drain off the oil that the tuna's packed in and add a little of the best olive oil you can afford. (I personally love a grassy Apulian or Tuscan variety.) No matter how expensive the tuna, a fresh splash of superior olive oil can really take this dish to another level.

Simple Crostini

When I first opened Bellini, we used to serve crostini gratis but eventually stopped because there came a point when all that the guests wanted were these addictive little toasts. My secret was sprinkling them with a bit of Parmigiano-Reggiano before they went into the oven. This is not exactly conventional, but it adds a layer of flavor to whatever topping you spoon onto them.

MAKES ABOUT 12

1 (12") baguette, sliced on a sharp bias

¾ cup extra-virgin olive oil

¼ cup grated Parmigiano-Reggiano or Grana Padano

Kosher salt and freshly ground black pepper

PREHEAT THE OVEN to 350°F. Arrange the bread slices on 1 or 2 baking sheets. Brush both sides of the bread generously with the oil. Top each with some cheese and season with salt and pepper. Bake for 15 to 20 minutes, until golden. Rotate the baking sheets 180 degrees halfway through the cooking time. Cooled crostini can be stored in an airtight container for a day or two.

chef tip

- If your bread is slightly stale, redeem it by toasting or grilling. Rub the toasted slices with a cut garlic clove and drizzle with some high-quality extra-virgin olive oil.

- For dinner parties, I like to offer my guests a selection of rolls with the entrée: Consider a French roll, a multigrain, and one studded with something interesting like olives, raisins, or walnuts. Serve them warm, wrapped in a napkin.

- To elevate your meal instantly, pack good-quality butter into a small ramekin and top with a sprinkle of fleur de sel or colored salt. Serve at room temperature.

Bresaola Purses

Bresaola—thin slices of salty, cured beef—is popular in Italy, but for some reason it hasn't caught on in the United States the way prosciutto has. Serve it and you'll come off as a food insider. Bresaola is typically served carpaccio-style in Italy—arrayed on a plate and topped with a mound of arugula. Since bresaola holds its shape and doesn't tear easily, I like to fold the slices into cute little purses. Use fancy, bamboo toothpicks to hold it all together.

SERVES 4 TO 6

¼ cup extra-virgin olive oil

4 teaspoons white wine vinegar

¼ teaspoon kosher salt

Freshly ground black pepper

½ English cucumber, peeled, seeded, and cut into 1" matchsticks

2 scallions, white and green parts, trimmed and finely chopped

2 cups baby arugula

12 slices bresaola (about 7 ounces)

WHISK TOGETHER the olive oil, vinegar, salt, and plenty of pepper in a medium bowl. Add the cucumber, scallions, and arugula and toss to coat evenly. Put a pinch of the salad mixture in the middle of each slice of bresaola. Gather up both ends of the bresaola around the salad and secure with a toothpick. Arrange on a small tray and serve.

donatella clicks

Don't use boring wooden toothpicks from a box or the ones with colored frills. Go for organic bamboo picks, like those sold on www.jpbrince.com. They are sturdy and extra long.

Farinata with Fontina and Rosemary

As a head judge on the Food Network's *The Next Iron Chef* and *Iron Chef America*, I've gotten to know some incredible food experts. One of the coolest is Anya Fernald, who is now one of my closest friends, despite the fact that I cook in heels and she cures her own meat (not to mentions butchers her own cows). In food circles, she's known as the food sustainability chick. I recently visited her beautiful Oakland, California, home after a spa day that involved an organic juice fast and a seriously painful massage. We decided we had been so good that we needed to be bad. So while I opened the wine, she made this savory pancake, for which she is locally famous, in her hand-built outdoor pizza oven. Mine may not taste *exactly* like Anya's, but it's delicious and addictive (not to mention soooo easy)—even more so topped with paper-thin slices of prosciutto and/or fontina.

SERVES 4

⅔ cup chickpea flour (also known as garbanzo bean flour)

½ teaspoon fine sea salt

3 tablespoons extra-virgin olive oil

Needles from a small sprig of fresh rosemary

Kosher salt and freshly ground black pepper

1–2 ounces fontina cheese and/or prosciutto, cut into slivers

COMBINE THE FLOUR with ¾ cup water in a bowl, and whisk with a metal whisk until it is smooth. Whisk in the sea salt and 2 tablespoons of the olive oil. Let sit at room temperature for at least 4 hours.

PREHEAT THE OVEN to 450°F.

SWIRL THE REMAINING 1 TABLESPOON OF OLIVE OIL in an 11" cast-iron or ovenproof nonstick skillet. Place in the hot oven for 10 minutes. Pour all of the batter into the hot pan and swirl so that the batter reaches up the sides of the pan by ¼". Scatter the rosemary on the surface and bake about 15 minutes, until the lacy edges begin to darken and the underside is golden. Immediately sprinkle with a pinch of kosher salt and plenty of pepper. Slide the pancake onto a cutting board. Top with the fontina and/or prosciutto, cut into eighths, and serve hot.

Grilled Swordfish and Watermelon Skewers

I've been lucky enough to work with chef Michael Psilakis, whose talent for unusual ingredient combinations and modern takes on his Greek culinary heritage shot him to stardom. These fish, cheese, and fruit skewers were inspired by a dish on the menu at Anthos that blew me away.

Cut all of the ingredients into cubes of the same size, not only because it looks good, but because they need to lie on the ridges of the grill pan at the same time to cook evenly. Thread the ingredients onto 8" skewers, weighting them to one end so that guests can hold them comfortably.

MAKES 14 SKEWERS, SERVES 4 TO 6

YOU'LL NEED: cast-iron stovetop grill pan

1 pound seedless watermelon, cut into 1" cubes or ½ pound precut seedless watermelon cubes

7 ounces Manouri or halloumi cheese, cut into 1" cubes

7–8 ounces swordfish steak, 1" thick, cut into 1" cubes

Extra-virgin olive oil, for brushing

Kosher salt and freshly ground black pepper

Dried oregano

Juice of ½ lemon

HEAT A CAST-IRON STOVETOP GRILL PAN OVER HIGH HEAT.

THREAD THE CUBES of watermelon, cheese, and swordfish onto each bamboo skewer, alternating attractively. (When threading the cheese, press gently while twisting back and forth to prevent the cube from splitting.) Make sure the flat sides are aligned.

BRUSH ONE SIDE OF EACH SKEWER with a little olive oil, and season with salt, pepper, and oregano. Place the skewers in the grill pan so that the oiled sides make full contact with the hot surface. Grill for 2 minutes without moving the skewers. While you're waiting, brush the top of each skewer with the olive oil and season with additional salt, pepper, and oregano. Turn off the heat and carefully turn each skewer over, without allowing the cubes to shift or turn. Grill over the residual heat until the swordfish is firm, about 2 minutes more. Transfer to a platter and drizzle all over with the lemon juice.

donatella clicks

If your cheesemonger doesn't carry Manouri, beg him to start! Otherwise, check out www.christosmarket.com for all things Greek.

Mini Caprese

One of my fondest summer memories of Italy is going to the market in Torrito with my aunt Rosinella, who always felt the compulsion to introduce me as the American! Shopping at the farmers' market in Union Square in New York City when the heirloom tomatoes are at their peak always brings me back to Torrito.

You will recognize the combination of ingredients here—mozzarella, tomatoes, and basil. I've just put them onto a bamboo skewer. I make these as often as possible until the fresh tomatoes disappear in the early fall. They keep me in summer mode just a little bit longer. Other great partners for skewers: squares of Brie and slender pear slices; seedless watermelon chunks, Greek feta, and pitted Kalamata olives. Because there's no cooking involved, make it your business to buy top-notch fleur de sel and extra-virgin olive or truffle oil.

MAKES ABOUT 10 SKEWERS, SERVES 4 TO 6

1 pound red or yellow cherry or pear tomatoes, preferably heirloom

1 cup small basil leaves

1 pound bocconcini, packed in water

Extra-virgin olive oil or truffle oil

Fleur de sel

THREAD A TOMATO ONTO A SKEWER, followed by a basil leaf and a bocconcino. Repeat with a second tomato, basil leaf, and bocconcino. Repeat with the remaining ingredients; you should have 10 skewers in all. Arrange the skewers on a large platter. Just before serving, drizzle with a little olive or truffle oil and season with fleur de sel.

donatella clicks

Fleur de sel is the caviar of salts. Hailing from Brittany, France, it's de rigueur in a good cook's pantry. If you can't find it locally, order it from www.faeriesfinest.com or www.igourmet.com.

Seafood Salad in Radicchio Cups

At my first restaurant, Bellini, the chilled seafood salad sold out every summer day. I eventually realized why: Everyone loves it but *no one* wants to make it at home. The peeling. The cleaning. The trimming. I confess that, back then, when I entertained at home, I took the sneaky route by bringing the salad home, undressed, from the restaurant, then tossing it in a homemade vinaigrette and passing it off as my own. You can do the same—just ask your fish seller for seafood salad with no dressings or anything else binding it together. Always ask exactly what type of seafood is in the salad in case any guest has allergies.

One caveat: While I may encourage a little cheating, I draw the line at bottled dressings. If you don't have time to make this fabulous vinaigrette, just use a little good-quality olive oil, red wine vinegar, and salt and pepper.

SERVES 4 TO 6

½ fennel bulb, trimmed of stalks and any discolored areas and quartered lengthwise

½ pound top-quality mixed seafood salad, each piece sliced ⅛" thick

1 shallot, very finely chopped

1 celery stalk, finely chopped

1 tablespoon finely snipped chives

1 tablespoon chopped flat-leaf parsley

1½ tablespoons white or black truffle oil

1½ teaspoons fresh lemon juice

1½ teaspoons mayonnaise

Kosher salt and freshly ground black pepper

1 large or 2 medium heads radicchio, outer and blemished leaves removed

1 tablespoon capers, drained

QUARTER THE FENNEL BULB and trim away most of the fennel's core. Slice the fennel paper-thin, crosswise, then chop coarsely. Combine the fennel, seafood, shallot, celery, chives, and parsley in a bowl. Add the truffle oil, lemon juice, mayonnaise, ¼ teaspoon salt, and plenty of pepper. Mix gently with a fork until evenly blended. Season with more salt and pepper to taste. The salad can be refrigerated, covered, for up to 4 hours.

SEPARATE THE LARGEST OUTER LEAVES OF THE RADICCHIO carefully, keeping them as intact as possible. You should have about 20 cupped leaves (save the smaller, inner leaves for another salad). Arrange the cups on a platter. Use 2 forks to mound about 2 tablespoons of the salad into each radicchio cup. Garnish each with a few capers. The salads may be refrigerated, covered, for up to 1 hour. Let stand at room temperature for about 10 minutes before serving to allow the flavors to wake up.

Zucchini alla Scapece

My mother served this classic peasant dish at every occasion, formal or informal, because she could prepare it first thing in the morning and let the zucchini cure while she devoted her attention to the main meal—the longer it sits, the better it is. The zucchini are so insanely good that when my friend renowned antitrust attorney Lloyd Constantine called me in a panic for suggestions of what to cook for his dear friends Tim and Nina Zagat, of restaurant guide renown, I gave him this recipe. It turned out to be the most successful dish at his party!

I doubt there will be leftovers, but if there are, sandwich them between 2 slices of rustic Italian bread or serve them with eggs for breakfast.

SERVES 4 TO 6

¼ cup red wine vinegar

1 large garlic clove, chopped

Kosher salt and freshly ground black pepper

8 mint leaves plus more for garnish

Olive oil for frying

3 medium green zucchini, or a mix of yellow and green zucchini, sliced on the diagonal into ¼" rounds

COMBINE THE VINEGAR, GARLIC, AND ¼ TEASPOON EACH SALT AND PEPPER IN A SMALL BOWL. Submerge the mint leaves in it and set aside.

FILL A LARGE SKILLET WITH ¼" OLIVE OIL and heat over medium-high heat. When the oil is hot but not smoking, slide the zucchini slices into the pan in a single layer. Do not overcrowd. Fry about 7 minutes, until golden and flecked with dark spots, flipping constantly with a fork. Transfer the zucchini slices to a platter, overlapping them.

REMOVE THE MINT LEAVES from the vinegar mixture and cut in thin slices. Drizzle the vinegar mixture over the zucchini, scatter with the mint strands, and season with more salt and pepper. Set aside at room temperature for at least 20 minutes and as long as 8 hours. Garnish with fresh mint leaves.

chef tip: making herbs into pretty little ribbons

If you learn one knife skill, make it this one. Basil, mint, and other soft herbs bruise if you chop them randomly, so chefs gently slice them into strands, called chiffonade. To do this, stack the leaves on top of one another. Roll them up as you would a cigarette. Using a sharp paring knife, cut the roll on an angle into thin strips. Separate each bundle into individual strips and use for garnish.

Greek Pizzette

I'll be honest with you, unless I have a party coming up, my refrigerator isn't exactly overflowing. Maybe you can relate? This is partly because I'm always at the restaurants, and I tend to wind up eating whatever the chefs can toss together while they're closing the kitchen. One night, with barely any effort, Michael Psilakis did what comes so naturally to him: He tapped into his Greek culinary roots and took off from there. These little pizzas are, honestly, to die for.

SERVES 4

4 pocketless pitas

½ cup extra-virgin olive oil

½ cup fig jam

½ pound halloumi cheese, cut into ¼" slices

2 cups baby arugula

Juice of 1 lemon

2 teaspoons dried oregano

Kosher salt and freshly ground black pepper

4 fresh figs, halved lengthwise

PREHEAT THE OVEN to 350°F.

BRUSH BOTH SIDES OF THE PITAS with ¼ cup of the olive oil and place on a baking sheet. Bake about 10 minutes, until golden and crisp. Let cool slightly.

MEANWHILE, TURN ON THE BROILER and set the rack 6" from the heat source. Spread the pitas with the fig jam, then top each with some halloumi. Slide the pitas under the broiler for about 3 minutes, until the halloumi is melted.

PUT THE ARUGULA IN A LARGE BOWL, add the lemon juice and remaining ¼ cup olive oil, and toss to thoroughly coat all of the leaves. Season with the oregano, salt, and pepper. Divide the arugula among the pitas. Top each with two fig halves. Arrange on a platter, and serve.

Pear and Cinnamon Compote with a Selection of Cheeses

Several years back, celebrated chef and dear friend Scott Conant opened his first Manhattan restaurant to great acclaim. Today I visit him at Scarpetta. I don't know if he was the first to serve a cheese course with jams and compotes in New York, but I do remember it becoming a trend soon after his won raves. This particular compote I created is fragrant with cinnamon and pears, just the aromas you want to greet your guests at a fall party. Cooking apples, such as Granny Smiths, can be substituted for the pears. The compote is perfect, too, with grilled sausages. For added drama, nix the tired wood platter and serve on mirrored glass.

MAKES ENOUGH TO SPREAD ON 24 TOASTED BAGUETTE SLICES

2 ripe Bosc, Bartlett, or Comice pears, peeled, quartered, cored, and coarsely chopped

1 cinnamon stick

2½ tablespoons fruity white wine, such as Riesling

1 tablespoon granulated sugar, or to taste

12 ounces total of a combination of soft pecorino cheese, Gorgonzola, and ricotta salata, sliced in wedges

Toasted baguette slices or large crackers

Artisanal honey, for drizzling, with honeycomb

COMBINE THE PEARS, CINNAMON, WINE, AND SUGAR in a skillet over medium-low heat. Bring to a gentle simmer and cook about 12 minutes, stirring occasionally, until the pears are almost falling apart. Let cool to warm room temperature. Transfer the compote to a food processor and pulse until slightly chunky. The compote may be covered and refrigerated for up to 8 hours; bring to room temperature before serving.

TRANSFER THE COMPOTE to a serving bowl and place on a large platter. Arrange the cheeses and baguette slices around the compote. Put a bit of honeycomb on each slice of cheese. Invite guests to layer a slice of cheese and dollop of compote on the baguette slices.

Gorgonzola Dolce, Bacon, and Onion Crostini

I'm unapologetically from the everything-tastes-better-on-bread school. Unlike the other crostinis in this book, this one requires a bit of cooking—the warm bacon and onion mixture wilts the frisée just enough to make for easy piling on top of the crostini. Gorgonzola dolce is a milder, creamier version of Gorgonzola cheese, which is fine to use in its place. Serve on slate boards. I found these at Pottery Barn.

MAKES 12
CROSTINI,
SERVES 4 TO 6

8 ounces Gorgonzola dolce, at room temperature

1 small head frisée, trimmed to the yellow leaves

¼ pound smoked bacon, diced

½ small red onion, thinly sliced

¼ cup sherry vinegar

Kosher salt and freshly ground black pepper

Simple Crostini (page 22)

2 teaspoons fresh thyme leaves

BEAT THE GORGONZOLA using an electric mixer until it is light and fluffy. Set aside. Place the frisée in a heatproof bowl and set aside.

COOK THE BACON OVER MEDIUM HEAT just until most of the fat is rendered. Do not over-cook. Remove to a plate with a slotted spoon. Add the onion to the fat in the pan and cook for 10 to 15 minutes, until it begins to caramelize. Add the vinegar and cook, scraping up the bits on the bottom of the pan with a wooden spoon, until the vinegar evaporates. Pour the mixture over the frisée, add the bacon, and toss. Season to taste with salt and pepper.

ARRANGE THE CROSTINI ON A PLATTER. Spread a thin layer of the cheese on each. Top with the bacon-frisée mixture, garnish with the thyme leaves, and serve.

WINTER
COCKTAIL
PARTY

Cocktail parties are the ideal way to entertain in the wintertime, providing the perfect format for ringing in the holidays! Consider a tree-trimming party or New Year's Eve party

SETTING THE SCENE

YOUR SPACE SHOULD SPARKLE for a cocktail party. Candlelight, of course, is a no-brainer for achieving this, but throw glass, white ceramics, and metallics into the mix and it gives those flames a lot to bounce off of. So elegant. I use a mix of modern and traditional tableware—my pretty clear tumblers for serving artisanal jams, minimalist ceramic trays, and my grandmother's gold-handled porcelain espresso cups for dainty portions of soup. One of the greatest favors you can do for yourself is to buy a couple dozen ceramic appetizer spoons. Look on restaurant supply Web sites like www.jbprince.com or check out the French ceramic houses if you want to add a little gold or silver bling to your spread. Once you have them, you'll find you want to miniaturize every dish in this book—and serve them on these spoons! And to really give the table an air of elegance, use super-tall candlesticks or candles—they're unexpected in the age of votives everywhere and push your cool quotient off the charts. (Shop www.westelm.com and www.LBZ.com for inexpensive candlesticks.)

WHAT TO POUR

A signature cocktail, a red wine, white wine, basic liquors and a special dessert wine

SIGNATURE COCKTAIL • Prosecco with a splash of cranberry juice and garnished with skewered, sugared cranberries

RED WINE • A pinot noir is always a safe bet; it is gentle enough to pair with seafood yet has enough backbone to stand up to charcuterie. One of my favorites is Willamette Valley Pinot Noir from Oregon.

WHITE WINE • A good sauvignon blanc is among my favorite white grape varietals to serve for cocktail hour. It's the ultimate versatile wine. La Doucette, a Sancerre from the

Loire Valley, is a staple in my wine cellar, as is Cloudy Bay Sauvignon Blanc from New Zealand.

DESSERT WINE • I love to serve port with a bit of chocolate as the cocktail party winds down. My favorite producer is Fonseca, justly famous for its rich and warm yet intensely fruity port.

DURING THE HOLIDAYS, I can't help but play Christmas music at my cocktail parties. I love Nat King Cole, Bing Crosby, Louis Armstrong (okay, I'm a hopeless romantic), and Vince Guaraldi, but I also make sure to mix in modern artists such as Pink Martini. Refrain from playing choral music.

WHAT TO WEAR

LIKE THE SETTING ITSELF, you should sparkle—but not too much. We all have our little black dresses, but I have found that whenever I go for color, I invariably get more compliments! If you opt for black, make it dramatic—one shoulder, backless—you get the picture. And of course, a great pair of heels. Holidays are not the time to wear practical pumps! Go easy on the jewelry; sometimes a statement-making cocktail ring and unassuming earrings are enough. Treat yourself to a blow-out and mani-pedi—you deserve it!

My go-to shopping sources are net-a-porter (www.netaporter.com) and its outlet version, www.outnet.com. Look for high-end dresses and shoes, with next-day delivery.

RESTAURANT INSIDER TIP
speed rack

Take a tip from your favorite bartender and set up a speed rack. It's simply a lineup of one bottle of the most-requested liquor—vodka, gin, tequila, rum—and one bottle of each type of mixer—sour mix, tonic, soda water, cranberry and orange juices. A bartender places it directly in front of where he/she does the most bartending so that the drink making goes quickly. Arrange small glasses full of garnishes such as lime and lemon wedges and twists and olives nearby.

chapter two SOUPS, SALADS, *and* SMALL PLATES

Winter

Roasted Baby Beet Salad with Pistachios

Zia Laura's Soup

Cannellini Bean Soup with Fried Sage

Pear and Parsnip Soup

Winter White Salad

Spring

Garlic Soup with Swirled Beets

Mussels with Fregola and Pesto

Herb-Tied Salad

Burrata with Blood Oranges and Fennel

Tomato-Cucumber Salad

Summer

Bocconcini with Peaches

Heirloom Tomato Panzanella

Zucchini Fritters

Eggplant Napoleon

Cucumber Soup with Crab, Yogurt, and Dill

Fall

Lentil Soup with Shrimp and Bacon

Gennaro's Black Kale Salad with Currants

Autumn Squash Soup with Pumpkin Seeds and Star Anise

Roasted Diver Scallops with Brown Butter Sauce

Zia Donata's Fava Bean Puree with Swiss Chard

Putting together a menu of several small plates is one of my favorite ways to entertain. It's also the way I like to eat, perhaps a reflection of my heritage, my lifestyle, and my career, which demands that I keep up with food trends. In Puglia, the minute you sit down in any small restaurant, waiters parade from the kitchen with a meal's worth of tasting dishes. I usually end up skipping the main course in favor of sampling from each one. In New York, most of my food-savvy friends rarely have sit-down dinners with plated courses, much preferring to indulge in what seems like an endless tasting menu. It brings to mind a recent party—one of the best I've been to in a long time. A Spanish friend and wonderful cook first set out a delicious selection of briny tinned seafood from Galicia that he had ordered online (yes, all he needed to do was open the cans!), sautéed slices of chorizo, Marcona almonds, and spiced olives, followed by mini chilled gazpacho in shot glasses, traditional tomato toasts, empanadas, and patatas bravas. There was also fig compote with Manchego cheese and plenty of sangria. The sheer number of dishes could make anyone quake in her high heels, but the truth is, few of them required anything more than a little clever assembly.

The point is, you should consider the recipes in this chapter as more than just the dishes you serve before the main course. Though they are perfect for that, almost every one of them can be assigned a new role, whether it's Autumn Squash Soup or Pear and Parsnip Soup that become hors d'oeuvres when you serve them in shot glasses or teacups, or Heirloom Tomato Panzanella and Cucumber Soup with Crab that are perfect for lunch. In the same way, many of the hors d'oeuvres in the previous chapter make great cross-dressers—they can easily become first courses or small plates depending on how you present them.

The dishes that follow provide an excellent snapshot of my split food personality: I'll always have one foot in my aunts' Puglian kitchens and the other behind the stoves of my restaurants. Burrata with Blood Oranges, Bocconcini with Peaches, and Lentil Soup with Shrimp and Bacon are perfect examples of the line my culinary leanings straddle.

As with every dish you cook, drama should always play a big part in these starters. Sometimes, it is inherent in the ingredients themselves, as in the sexy Winter White Salad, or the spectacle lies in the presentation (think Eggplant Napoleon and Herb-Tied Salad). For soups, there's nothing like pouring the servings into bowls from a big pitcher right at the table—my favorite way to serve Garlic Soup with Swirled Beets and Zia Laura's pretty vegetable soup. In fact, any chance you get, you should perform—snip herbs onto salads, drizzle sauces onto plates, drizzle extra-virgin olive oil from a gorgeous decanter into smooth soups, and ceremoniously season platters with exotic colored salt and pepper.

Roasted Baby Beet Salad with Pistachios

The concept for my restaurant Mia Dona was pretty simple: I wanted a place where I could eat the foods that my mother made for me as a child but add a little kick—in this case the cheese—wherever possible. This reinterpretation of the classic walnuts and blue cheese combination has been on the menu from the start. I come by my love of pistachios honestly—from my time spent in Sicily, where the world's best are grown. Fourme d'Ambert, my favorite blue cheese, has an earthy aroma but it is, in fact, quite mild. (See photo page 44.)

SERVES 4 TO 6

20–24 baby red, golden, or candy stripe beets, scrubbed

1 cup extra-virgin olive oil

Kosher salt and freshly ground black pepper

¼ cup red wine vinegar

1 tablespoon Dijon mustard

½ cup crumbled Fourme d'Ambert or other high-quality blue cheese

¼ cup toasted pistachios (below)

1 tablespoon fresh tarragon leaves plus sprigs for garnish

PREHEAT THE OVEN to 350°F. Toss the beets in ½ cup of the olive oil and season with salt and pepper. Wrap in aluminum foil and place on a baking sheet. Roast until the beets are easily pierced with a fork and the skin is easy to remove, about 1 hour. When the beets are cool enough to handle, peel and put them in a bowl. Cover and refrigerate.

WHISK TOGETHER THE VINEGAR and the mustard, slowly adding the remaining ½ cup olive oil until it is thoroughly incorporated. Season with salt and pepper to taste.

COMBINE THE BEETS, blue cheese, pistachios, and tarragon leaves in a large bowl. Toss with the vinaigrette. To serve, spoon onto individual plates or a rimmed platter and garnish with tarragon sprigs.

chef tip: how to toast just a few nuts

Toast the nuts in a dry skillet over medium-high heat, shaking the pan often, until just beginning to color, 4 to 5 minutes. Transfer to a bowl to cool.

Zia Laura's Soup

My mother's sister Laura has the touch. The oldest of the brood often turns the humblest ingredients into delicious, gorgeous food. This soup is a perfect example—zucchini, carrots, and leeks simmer in a simple broth, and the results are beyond satisfying. My vegan friends rejoice when I serve this dish! Grating the vegetables is key; if you cut them into chunks, it's more Tuesday night supper than Saturday evening dinner.

SERVES 4 TO 6

¼ cup extra-virgin olive oil

1 medium onion, chopped

2 leeks, white part only, root end trimmed, halved lengthwise, and cut into ½" pieces

Kosher salt and freshly ground black pepper

3 medium zucchini, grated on the large holes of a box grater

3 carrots, peeled and grated on the large holes of a box grater

1 (13-ounce) can whole plum tomatoes, drained of their juices and coarsely chopped

6 cups low-sodium beef or vegetable broth

4 basil leaves, green or purple, plus 4 sprigs for garnish

1 tablespoon coarsely chopped flat-leaf parsley

Parmigiano-Reggiano, grated or shaved in curls

HEAT THE OLIVE OIL in a medium pot over medium heat. Add the onion and leeks and sauté about 3 minutes, until soft and golden. Season with salt and pepper. Add the zucchini and carrots and sauté until softened, about 5 minutes more. Add the tomatoes, broth, 4 basil leaves, and parsley and bring to a boil. Cover the pot, reduce the heat to low, and simmer for 25 minutes. Serve with the grated Parmigiano on the side or garnished with the curls. Add a little purple basil for added drama.

Cannellini Bean Soup with Fried Sage

I always have eggs, juice, and cheese in the refrigerator—and like any good Italian, cannellini beans in the cupboard. On their own, cannellini are the plain Janes of the pantry, but with a little help from porcini broth and white wine, they make an earthy, complex soup. Fried sage, which shows up everywhere on the Italian table, just may be the world's most delicious garnish.

SERVES 4 TO 6

YOU'LL NEED: immersion blender, blender, or food processor

5 tablespoons extra-virgin olive oil

1 large onion, finely chopped

7 garlic cloves, finely chopped

½ teaspoon red-pepper flakes

1 cup dry white wine or vermouth

2 (15-ounce) cans cannellini beans, drained and rinsed

1 quart porcini broth (from 2 bouillon cubes, see Donatella Clicks), low-sodium vegetable broth, or chicken broth

¾ teaspoon kosher salt

Freshly ground black pepper

2 tablespoons unsalted butter

20 large fresh sage leaves, completely dry

1 (15-ounce) can Italian plum tomatoes, drained, seeded, and diced

WARM 3 TABLESPOONS OF THE OLIVE OIL in a large pot over medium heat. Add the onion and sauté until softened, about 3 minutes. Add the garlic and red-pepper flakes and cook until fragrant, about 30 seconds. Add the wine and simmer until it has evaporated. Add the beans, porcini broth, salt, and a generous grinding of pepper. Bring to a simmer, partially cover, and cook for 15 minutes. Turn off the heat and let stand for 5 minutes.

PUREE THE BEANS IN THE POT with an immersion blender or in batches in a blender or food processor until smooth. Keep warm.

WARM THE BUTTER and remaining 2 tablespoons of olive oil in a skillet over medium-high heat. Add the sage and cook, tossing, for about 2 minutes, until crisp.

LADLE THE SOUP into bowls and top with diced tomatoes and sage leaves.

donatella clicks

If you have trouble finding porcini bouillon cubes, they are available at many specialty grocers and online at www.italybymail.com.

Pear and Parsnip Soup

Pairing the lowly parsnip with the elegant pear is a lot like your insanely happily married friends who are not an obvious couple—the combination is sublime. While I'm not a big fan of cream-based soups, the cream is essential for carrying—and enhancing—the flavor here. I like to serve this elegant soup in teacups; the handles mean guests don't require a spoon. I raided my mom's cupboard for dainty teacups from my great-aunt Angela. For added drama, I sprinkle black salt into the beautiful creamy white soup.

SERVES 4 TO 6

YOU'LL NEED:
food processor, immersion blender, small strainer

2 tablespoons extra-virgin olive oil

2 shallots, thinly sliced

1¼ pounds parsnips, peeled and cut into ¾" chunks

¾ teaspoon kosher salt

White pepper, preferably freshly ground

3 cups low-sodium chicken or vegetable broth

2 ripe pears such as Bosc, Bartlett, or Comice

1 cup heavy cream

Black sea salt, for garnish

HEAT THE OLIVE OIL in a saucepan over medium-high heat. Add the shallots and sauté about 3 minutes, until soft and fragrant. Add the parsnips and cook for 5 minutes. Season with the salt and plenty of pepper. Add the broth and bring to a simmer, then partially cover and cook until the parsnips are tender, about 15 minutes. Meanwhile, peel, core, and cut the pears into large chunks. Puree in a food processor until smooth and set aside.

USING AN IMMERSION BLENDER, puree the parsnip mixture until smooth. Add the cream and simmer for 5 minutes more. Ladle the soup into bowls and swirl a spoonful of the pear puree into each. Garnish with the black salt and serve hot.

Winter White Salad

My dad and I created this salad together for my first restaurant, Bellini, where he spent a lot of time hanging around telling me what I didn't know. It embodies a modern cook's aesthetic: sophisticated, without much adornment because it's fabulous all on its own. Make sure the vegetables are chilled, as well as the plates and the vinaigrette, so that the salad stays crisp to the last bite.

SERVES 4 TO 6

Vinaigrette

¼ cup extra-virgin olive oil

2 tablespoons lemon extra-virgin olive oil

2 tablespoons fresh lemon juice

2 teaspoons Dijon mustard

½ teaspoon sea salt

Freshly ground black pepper

Salad

1 large fennel bulb, trimmed, halved, cored, and thinly sliced crosswise

2 endives, root ends trimmed and leaves separated

3 long pieces hearts of palm, from a can or jar, halved crosswise and cut into matchsticks

6 ounces white mushrooms, brushed clean and sliced

3 ounces imported Parmigiano-Reggiano or Grana Padano

CHILL 4 to 6 plates.

TO MAKE THE VINAIGRETTE: Whisk together the olive oils, lemon juice, mustard, salt, and a generous grinding of pepper in a small bowl.

TO MAKE THE SALAD: Gently toss the fennel, endives, hearts of palm, and mushrooms with the vinaigrette in a small bowl until evenly coated. Transfer to the chilled plates and, using a vegetable peeler, shave several curls of Parmigiano over the top of each salad. Serve immediately.

Garlic Soup with Swirled Beets

The first time I tasted Jean-Georges Vongerichten's now-legendary young garlic soup, I was not only blown away by the subtle flavor, but really taken with the presentation. It was served tableside, with the soup poured from pretty creamware pitchers. The drama made an indelible impression on me, and I've served my version à la Jean-Georges, but with a twist, at dinner parties ever since. When the mellow garlic broth (it's so mild you can kiss without apologies afterward) hits the beets in the bowl, a gorgeous ruby swirl emerges.

SERVES 4 TO 6

YOU'LL NEED: steamer insert, potato ricer or food mill, food processor

2 russet (baking) potatoes, peeled and quartered

1 large red beet, scrubbed, peeled, and cut into ¼"-thick slices

6 garlic cloves, sliced

⅓ cup white wine vinegar

⅓ cup extra-virgin olive oil

1 teaspoon kosher salt

Cracked black pepper

Torn mint leaves for garnish

PUT THE POTATOES in a small pot and add water to cover them by 1". Salt the water, cover, and cook over high heat 20 to 25 minutes, until the potatoes are fork tender.

MEANWHILE, IN A SAUCEPAN fitted with a steamer insert, steam the beets over simmering water until not quite tender, about 14 minutes. Cut into small dice.

REMOVE THE POTATOES from the pot with a slotted spoon and reserve the cooking water. Push the potatoes through a ricer or a food mill fitted with the largest disk into a saucepan and set aside. Puree the garlic and vinegar in a small food processor until very smooth. Stir it into the potatoes and add the olive oil, salt, and plenty of pepper. Add just enough of the reserved cooking water (¼ to ½ cup) to create an applesauce-like consistency. Bring to a simmer, then remove from the heat. Pour into a large heatproof pitcher.

TO SERVE, SPOON SOME DICED BEETS into each soup bowl and set at each guest's place. Pour the hot soup over and garnish with mint. Let your guests swirl away!

Mussels with Fregola and Pesto

Fregola is a grainlike Italian pasta very similar to Israeli couscous, except with a more complex flavor because it is toasted. It's not available at the local supermarket, but it's worth tracking down at an Italian grocer or specialty food shop. Think of this dish as the urbane relative of the classic pairing of mussels and bread; the fregola soaks up the mussel juices for you.

SERVES 4 TO 6

1 cup fregola or Israeli couscous

⅓ cup extra-virgin olive oil plus a little extra for the fregola

2 pounds cultivated mussels, well rinsed and scrubbed

4 garlic cloves, finely chopped

½ teaspoon dried oregano

¼ teaspoon red-pepper flakes

1 cup dry white wine

1 tablespoon roughly chopped flat-leaf parsley

1 tablespoon roughly chopped dill

1 tablespoon slivered basil

6 tablespoons very cold unsalted butter, cut into chunks

½ cup best-quality store-bought pesto from the refrigerator section

½ teaspoon kosher salt

½ teaspoon freshly ground black pepper

1 teaspoon fresh lemon juice

2 ounces ricotta salata, shaved with a vegetable peeler

BRING A LARGE POT of salted water to a boil. Add the fregola and cook for 8 to 10 minutes, until tender. Drain well in a colander and toss with a little olive oil to prevent it from sticking together.

WARM ⅓ CUP OF THE OLIVE OIL in a large saucepan with a tight-fitting lid over medium-low heat. Add the mussels, garlic, oregano, and red-pepper flakes. Cook for 2 to 3 minutes, until the garlic is softened and fragrant. Add the white wine and half the parsley, dill, and basil. Cover the pan and cook, shaking it every minute or so to distribute the mussels in the pan so that they cook evenly.

WHEN THE MUSSEL shells have opened (about 6 minutes), remove the pan from the heat and add the butter, fregola, pesto, salt, pepper, lemon juice, and remaining parsley, dill, and basil. Cover the pan and shake again to distribute all the ingredients evenly. Discard any mussels that have not opened. It means they are not good! To serve, ladle into large bowls with plenty of the broth and fregola and garnish with the ricotta salata.

Herb-Tied Salad

This is a very simple salad that could just as easily be tossed in a big wooden bowl, but where's the drama in that? Wrapped in lettuce leaves and tied with chives, the salad looks like you went to great lengths to make it—exactly the impression you want to make. Snip the herbs tableside onto each guest's plate to gain even more points for fabulousness. These pretty little packets can be all but destroyed if there's even a trace of grit in the lettuce, so be sure to wash it thoroughly (see Clean Greens, page 81).

SERVES 4 TO 6

1 small shallot, very finely chopped

1 teaspoon Dijon mustard

2 teaspoons white wine vinegar

2 tablespoons extra-virgin olive oil

¼ teaspoon kosher salt

Freshly ground black pepper

1 small head red or green leaf lettuce, or Lollo Rosso, washed and dried

5 ounces baby romaine, spring, or mesclun mix

4–6 long fresh chives

Small bouquet of fresh soft herbs such as dill, Italian parsley, chervil, and/or additional chives and edible flowers for garnish

WHISK THE SHALLOT, mustard, vinegar, olive oil, salt, and plenty of pepper together in a medium bowl. Separate 4 to 6 medium, canoe-shaped leaves of the leaf lettuce to serve as wraps for the salads. (Reserve the remaining lettuce for another use.)

ADD THE BABY ROMAINE MIX to the dressing and toss to coat thoroughly. Place a spoonful of the greens in each lettuce "canoe" and belt it with a long chive tied in a knot on top.

PLACE THE BOUQUET of fresh herbs on the table in a small vase and invite guests to garnish their salads as they wish *or* snip the herbs onto their salads for them at the table.

Burrata with Blood Oranges and Fennel

Burrata means "buttered" in Italian. Need I say more? I *lived* on these gorgeous, buttery tasting, white balls of mozzarella filled with cream during my summers in Puglia, where the cheese is famous.

When I first opened Mia Dona, I had to have this cheese imported weekly. Now it is available at better cheese and gourmet shops. Use burrata within a day or two.

SERVES 4 TO 6

YOU'LL NEED:
Microplane zester

⅓ cup paper-thin slivers red onion

1 blood orange, scrubbed and patted dry

1 tablespoon fresh lemon juice

3 tablespoons extra-virgin olive oil

¼ teaspoon kosher salt

Freshly ground black pepper

½ small fennel bulb, trimmed, cored, and sliced crosswise into paper-thin slices

8 ounces burrata (1 or 2 balls) or buffalo mozzarella

1 teaspoon 25- or 50-year-old balsamic vinegar, for drizzling

1 tablespoon high-quality extra-virgin olive oil, for drizzling

Hawaiian sea salt (alea), for garnish (optional)

SOAK THE RED ONION in ice water for about 5 minutes. Meanwhile, remove the zest of the orange with a Microplane zester and set aside. Slice off the remaining peel and pith using a sharp knife, then cut down between the membranes to remove the fruit segments. Cut crosswise into chunks and set aside. Drain the red onion and spread on a paper towel to dry.

WHISK TOGETHER the lemon juice, 3 tablespoons olive oil, kosher salt, and plenty of pepper in a medium bowl. Add the red onion and fennel and toss to coat evenly. Place the pouch of burrata on a serving platter and break open to expose the creamy interior. (If using buffalo mozzarella, slice thickly and arrange on a platter.) Top with the red onion mixture and blood oranges, and drizzle sparingly with the balsamic vinegar and the high-quality olive oil. Garnish with the orange zest and a few grains of Hawaiian sea salt (if using).

donatella clicks

Hawaiian sea salt is made from salt crystals baked in Hawaiian red clay. You can use it as you would regular sea salt, to much more dramatic effect. Find it at Natural Sea Salts (www.naturalseasalts.com).

Tomato-Cucumber Salad

It wasn't chic, but the salad of tomatoes and cucumbers my mother made me growing up is still one of my favorites. She dressed it in olive oil and red wine vinegar and seasoned it with dried oregano. I've kept it the same, but created a pungent dressing to make it sing. Make the dressing an hour or so ahead of time, and keep all the vegetables refrigerated until just before you slice them.

SERVES 4 TO 6

Dressing

1 large garlic clove, smashed and very finely chopped

1 small shallot, very finely chopped

1 teaspoon Dijon mustard

1 tablespoon red wine vinegar

1 teaspoon balsamic vinegar

½ teaspoon dried oregano

½ teaspoon kosher salt

Freshly ground black pepper

3 tablespoons extra-virgin olive oil

1 tablespoon lemon extra-virgin olive oil

1 tablespoon finely chopped basil

Salad

1 seedless cucumber, peeled, seeded, and cut into chunks

6 plum tomatoes, seeded and cut into chunks

½ very small red onion, cut into thin slices lengthwise

⅔ cup Gaeta olives, pitted and halved

1 cup crumbled Greek feta (optional)

1½ cups (7-8 ounces) caperberries, drained

CHILL 4 to 6 salad plates.

TO MAKE THE DRESSING: Whisk together the garlic, shallot, mustard, red wine vinegar, balsamic vinegar, oregano, salt, plenty of pepper, and both olive oils, until smooth. Stir in the basil.

TO MAKE THE SALAD: Combine the cucumber, tomatoes, red onion, olives, and feta in a large, chilled bowl. Add the dressing and toss thoroughly. Fold in the caperberries. Arrange on the chilled plates and serve.

Bocconcini with Peaches

Italians don't really go for fruit in savory dishes, preferring to eat it fresh and whole after the evening meal. Though this combination of tiny balls of mozzarella and peaches may never have shown up on one of my Puglian aunts' tables, I can just hear them saying "Ahhhhh, l'Americana," and know they would come to love it although they wouldn't admit it. Fresh peaches are a must; if they're not ripe they obviously won't taste good *and* they won't come loose from the pit easily. Store any leftover bocconcini in the container you purchased them in, covered in water. I've made this salad on the fly without grilling the peaches and it is still very good.

SERVES 4 TO 6

YOU'LL NEED:
cast-iron
stovetop grill
pan

4 ripe peaches, halved, pitted, and each half cut into 3 wedges

1 pound bocconcini, packed in water

20 small basil leaves plus more for garnish

2 medium shallots, finely chopped

¼ cup extra-virgin olive oil

3 tablespoons balsamic vinegar

Sea salt and freshly ground black pepper

BRUSH A CAST-IRON STOVETOP GRILL PAN with a little olive oil and heat over high heat.

GRILL THE PEACH WEDGES about 2 to 3 minutes per side, until nicely charred. Transfer them to a large bowl and add the bocconcini, basil, shallots, olive oil, and vinegar. Toss gently until everything is well coated. Season with salt and pepper and set aside at room temperature for 15 minutes. Divide among salad plates or transfer to a rimmed platter. Garnish with the basil leaves and serve.

Heirloom Tomato Panzanella

It's a Tuscan peasant dish through and through: stale bread moistened with juicy tomatoes and olive oil. But with a little tweaking—colorful heirloom tomatoes, haricot verts, ricotta salata—this citified panzanella is posh enough to serve to your well-heeled friends without reservation.

SERVES 4 TO 6

Croutons

½ loaf rustic Italian bread, cut into 1" cubes

6 garlic cloves, minced

3 tablespoons dried oregano

¾ cup extra-virgin olive oil

Kosher salt and freshly ground black pepper to taste

Vinaigrette

3 tablespoons Dijon mustard

½ cup red wine vinegar

1 cup extra-virgin olive oil

Kosher salt and freshly ground black pepper to taste

Salad

1 pound haricot verts

2½ pounds (about 4 medium) assorted heirloom tomatoes, cored and each cut into 8 wedges

1 pound ricotta salata, shaved with a vegetable peeler

Sea salt and freshly ground black pepper

1 cup torn fresh basil leaves

TO MAKE THE CROUTONS: Preheat the oven to 300°F. Combine the bread, garlic, oregano, and olive oil in a large bowl and toss until the cubes are completely coated. Spread on a rimmed baking sheet in a single layer, season with salt and pepper, and bake for 15 to 20 minutes, until golden brown. Set aside to cool.

TO MAKE THE VINAIGRETTE: Combine the mustard and vinegar in a small bowl. Whisk in the olive oil in a slow, steady stream. Season to taste with salt and pepper.

TO MAKE THE SALAD: Bring a large pot of generously salted water to a boil. Prepare an ice bath. Blanch the haricots verts in the boiling water for 2 to 6 minutes, or until barely tender, with a slightly firm bite still left to them. Drain the beans and transfer to the ice bath to chill quickly, then drain again and dry on paper towels. Cut each in half. Combine the haricots verts and tomatoes in a large bowl. Shave the ricotta salata into the bowl using the large holes of a box grater. Add the croutons and toss to combine thoroughly. Pour the vinaigrette over the salad and croutons and gently toss with wooden spoons. Season with sea salt and pepper. Transfer the salad to a serving bowl or platter, garnish with the basil, and serve.

Zucchini Fritters

Proust had his madeleines; I have my zucchini fritters. One bite and I'm taken back to my Long Island grade school, where I was the only student with immigrant parents. I went by Donna in an attempt to assimilate, but instead of packing a PBJ in a Farrah Fawcett lunch box, my mother sent me off with foil-wrapped fritters stuffed into a brown paper bag. Despite the fact that I whined for a more mainstream lunch and was relentlessly picked on, I secretly *loooved* these. Today, I beg my mother to make them. Hers are without question the best, but mine are a pretty close second. She never grates the zucchini (which I am always tempted to do because it's quicker—alas, results in a watery batter), but rather cuts the zucchini into almost confetti-like pieces. The tinier the zucchini pieces, the better. Use a food processor with the fine-dice attachment for the best results, or cut by hand the way my mommy does it.

SERVES 4 TO 6

4 medium zucchini, finely diced

2 eggs, lightly beaten

2 tablespoons chopped flat-leaf parsley

½ cup grated Parmigiano-Reggiano

1 teaspoon extra-virgin olive oil

Kosher salt and freshly ground black pepper

¾–1 cup all-purpose flour

Olive oil

COMBINE THE ZUCCHINI, eggs, parsley, Parmigiano, and extra-virgin olive oil and stir until the zucchini is coated. Season generously with salt and pepper. Add ¾ cup of the flour just a sprinkle at a time and stir. Continue adding until the mix is the consistency of pancake batter, add more if the zucchini is very wet.

FILL A LARGE, HEAVY-BOTTOMED PAN with ¼" olive oil. Heat over medium heat until hot but not smoking. Working in batches, spoon the zucchini mixture into the pan in 2-tablespoon mounds. The fritters should be three-quarters submerged in the oil. If bits of zucchini stray, scoop them up and return them to the fritters. Reduce the heat slightly and fry until golden brown, turning once, about 5 minutes per side. Remove from the pan with a slotted spoon and drain on paper towels. Allow the oil to return to medium heat before proceeding with the next batch.

SERVE THE FRITTERS on a parchment-lined tray. The leftover fritters will keep, covered and refrigerated, up to 2 days. Reheat, wrapped in foil, in a low oven.

Eggplant Napoleon

It's not enough simply to cook with style; the food should be as stylish as you are. I must admit that even a bad eggplant Parmesan can taste good, but it isn't the kind of thing you want to serve guests. It's just not pretty. This is my modern take, stripped down to its essential, beautiful, delicious self.

SERVES 6

YOU'LL NEED:
cast-iron
stovetop grill
pan

2 Japanese eggplants, each cut into 4 diagonal slices

¼ cup balsamic vinegar

¾ cup extra-virgin olive oil

1 garlic clove, minced

3 tablespoons flat-leaf parsley, finely chopped

Kosher salt and freshly ground black pepper to taste

2 tablespoons red wine vinegar

3 or 4 small balls buffalo mozzarella, 14 ounces total, cut into thick slices

12 basil leaves plus more for garnish

2 tablespoons pine nuts, toasted (page 49)

SALT THE EGGPLANT and place in a colander to allow any excess liquid to drain off. Whisk together the balsamic vinegar, ½ cup of the olive oil, the garlic, parsley, salt, and pepper in a medium bowl. Add the eggplant and toss to coat. Set aside for 10 minutes.

BRUSH A CAST-IRON STOVETOP GRILL PAN with a thin layer of olive oil. Place over medium-high heat. Grill the eggplant until slightly charred, about 5 minutes per side. Set aside on a plate to cool. Meanwhile, make the vinaigrette. Put the red wine vinegar in a small bowl. Whisk in the remaining ¼ cup of olive oil in a steady stream.

TO BUILD THE NAPOLEON, begin with a slice of the eggplant, followed by a slice of mozzarella topped with a basil leaf. Repeat. Drizzle with the vinaigrette and garnish with the basil leaves. Scatter the pine nuts around each napoleon and serve.

Cucumber Soup with Crab, Yogurt, and Dill

This may sound like a ladies-who-lunch kind of soup, but it's far cooler than that. It has everything going for it: It's healthful, beautiful, and stylish. The soup itself is so refreshing you don't need the crab, but why not? Buy only fresh, fresh, fresh crabmeat—no canned or fake versions allowed.

SERVES 4 TO 6

YOU'LL NEED:
food processor or blender

1 English cucumber, ¾ peel removed, and cut into large chunks

1½ cups full-fat plain Greek yogurt

½ cup sour cream

1 shallot, grated or very finely chopped

¼ cup extra-virgin olive oil

2 tablespoons fresh dill fronds

¾ teaspoon kosher salt

Freshly ground white pepper

6 ounces lump crabmeat, broken up

Lemon olive oil, for drizzling (optional)

CHILL 4 to 6 shallow, rimmed soup bowls.

COMBINE THE CUCUMBER, yogurt, sour cream, shallot, olive oil, 1 tablespoon of the dill, the salt, and plenty of pepper in the bowl of a food processor or in a blender. Pulse, scraping down the sides with a rubber spatula, until completely smooth. Cover and refrigerate until ready to serve.

LADLE INTO THE CHILLED BOWLS and mound some crabmeat in the center. Garnish with the remaining dill and a drizzle of lemon olive oil if you'd like.

Lentil Soup with Shrimp and Bacon

The version of lentil soup made with bacon and carrots or potatoes is delicious, but it could use a little refinement if you're serving it to anyone but your family. Braising the lentils in red wine and adding succulent shrimp does the trick. If you plan to make this as a main course for 4, use the larger amount of shrimp.

SERVES 4 TO 6

YOU'LL NEED: blender, food processor, or immersion blender

2 teaspoons extra-virgin olive oil

1 tablespoon unsalted butter

4 ounces bacon, cut into matchstick strips

6–8 ounces medium shrimp, peeled, deveined, and cut crosswise in thirds

Kosher salt and freshly ground black pepper

1 small onion, finely chopped

2 celery ribs, finely chopped

5 garlic cloves, finely chopped

1 cup dried brown lentils

½ cup dry red wine

1 quart low-sodium chicken broth

½ teaspoon ground cumin

Snipped chives or slivered scallion greens, for garnish

WARM THE OLIVE OIL and butter in a large pot over medium-high heat. Add the bacon and cook until golden. Season the shrimp with salt and pepper and add to the pot. Cook, tossing occasionally, until pink, about 3 minutes. Transfer the shrimp and bacon to a plate with a slotted spoon.

ADD THE ONION, celery, and garlic to the pan and cook, tossing occasionally, until softened and golden, about 5 minutes. Add the lentils and stir to coat well. Add ¼ teaspoon salt and the wine and simmer until the wine has evaporated. Add the broth, stir in the cumin, and bring to a low simmer. Partially cover the pan and cook for 25 to 30 minutes, until the lentils are tender. Let cool for 5 minutes, then puree about half the soup in a blender or food processor. (Alternatively, use an immersion blender to puree it in the pot.) Return it to the pot and add the shrimp and bacon. Stir over low heat to warm through. To serve, ladle into bowls and garnish with a generous pinch of chives.

Gennaro's Black Kale Salad with Currants

I would love to say that this is my creation, but I happily throw the spotlight on my friend Gennaro Picione, the man behind the highly regarded Gennaro Restaurant on Manhattan's Upper West Side. On my first visit there, he brought out this salad, and I've been addicted ever since. It's all about the vincotto, a cooked Puglian wine made from dark, sweet, dense grapes. Substituting an aged balsamic vinegar just isn't the same. You won't find vincotto at the supermarket, but I urge you to track it down—at the local Italian grocer, specialty food shop, or online.

SERVES 4 TO 6

1 large bunch (about ½ pound) Tuscan kale (cavalo nero), center ribs and stems removed, leaves washed and cut in bite size pieces

¼ cup dried currants

½ cup extra-virgin olive oil

2 garlic cloves, chopped

1 teaspoon red-pepper flakes

2 tablespoons pine nuts, toasted (page 49)

Kosher salt and freshly ground black pepper

¼ cup vincotto

½ cup shaved ricotta salata

PUT THE KALE in a large bowl and set aside. Place the currants in another bowl and add hot water to cover. Let stand for 5 minutes to plump. Drain and pat dry.

HEAT THE OLIVE OIL in a small pot over medium heat. Add the garlic and cook until fragrant, about 1 minute; do not burn. Add the red-pepper flakes and cook for 30 seconds more. Add the kale and sauté for just a minute until it softens slightly. Remove from the heat. Add the pine nuts and currants, season with salt and pepper, and toss. Transfer immediately to salad plates, drizzle with the vincotto, and top with the ricotta salata.

donatella clicks

Vincotto will become one of your secret culinary weapons. I tend to use it whenever a recipe calls for deglazing the pan with red wine. Buon Italia (www.buonitalia.com) carries a variety of flavors including fig, lemon, and raspberry.

Autumn Squash Soup with Pumpkin Seeds and Star Anise

This soup is intensely aromatic, so much so that your guests will want to pretend they're sipping it by a fire after a day of skiing. Tying the spices up in the cheesecloth pouch is the key to infusing the soup with a hint of clove and star anise. I've served this for both formal and casual parties—it can go either way depending on what you serve it in. Peeling the squash takes some time so do it in advance if possible.

SERVES 4 TO 6

YOU'LL NEED: blender or immersion blender, cheesecloth

3 sprigs fresh thyme

4 whole cloves

1 star anise pod

1 teaspoon multicolored peppercorns

1 large butternut squash or 1¼ pounds frozen cubed squash

2 tablespoons extra-virgin olive oil plus extra for drizzling

3 shallots, thinly sliced

3 garlic cloves, thinly sliced

4 cups low-sodium chicken broth

¾ teaspoon kosher salt

Freshly ground black pepper

2 tablespoons orange blossom, clover, or lavender honey

2–3 tablespoons hulled pumpkin seeds (pepitas), toasted

PLACE THE THYME, cloves, star anise, and peppercorns in the center of a piece of cheesecloth and tie into a pouch. Set aside.

IF STARTING WITH A WHOLE SQUASH, use a vegetable peeler to remove all of the skin (it is very thick so be sure to get it all off) and halve the squash lengthwise. Remove the seeds and discard. Cut the squash into rough 1" chunks.

WARM THE OLIVE OIL in a large saucepan over medium heat. Add the shallots and garlic and cook about 2 minutes, until softened and fragrant. Add the squash, broth, salt, plenty of pepper, and the spice bag. Simmer, partially covered, until the squash is tender, 25 to 30 minutes for raw squash and 15 minutes for frozen.

REMOVE THE BAG of spices and puree the soup until super smooth with an immersion blender or in a blender. To serve, ladle into bowls, drizzle with the honey, and garnish with the pumpkin seeds and a final drizzle of extra-virgin olive oil.

Roasted Diver Scallops with Brown Butter Sauce

Your typical scallop entrée is the equivalent of a so-so date. It's "nice" and "interesting" but there's no spark. This dish was love at first bite. The dried cherries tart it up, but the real surprise is the cinnamon, a spice commonly used in savory Puglian dishes. Make sure the cauliflower is cut into tiny florets or they will not cook through. Diver scallops are hand-harvested rather than dredged, because dredging causes them to collect sand. Not only does harvesting scallops by hand protect undersea flora and fauna but, typically, they arrive at the market far sooner after being plucked from the water than do conventionally harvested scallops.

SERVES 4 TO 6

3 cups very small cauliflower florets

8–12 diver scallops

Kosher salt and freshly ground black pepper

2 tablespoons extra-virgin olive oil

¾ cup (1½ sticks) cold unsalted butter, cut into chunks

1 medium shallot, minced

12 fresh sage leaves

½ cup tart dried cherries

¼ teaspoon ground cinnamon

BRING A LARGE POT OF SALTED water to a boil. Add the cauliflower and cook about 3 minutes, until tender. Drain, spread on a kitchen towel, and pat dry.

PAT THE SCALLOPS DRY and season with salt and pepper. Heat 1 tablespoon of the olive oil in a large skillet over medium heat. Add the scallops and sear without moving for 2 minutes, until golden. Gently turn them over and add the butter, shallot, and sage to the pan. Cook until the scallops are just firm and translucent, about 2 minutes more. Divide the scallops among 4 to 6 salad plates using a slotted spoon. Set the skillet and the butter aside.

HEAT THE REMAINING 1 TABLESPOON of olive oil in another skillet over medium heat. Add the cauliflower and cherries and sauté, turning the cauliflower, until it is golden brown, 2 to 3 minutes. Sprinkle the cinnamon over the cauliflower mixture, season with the salt and pepper, and remove from the heat. Rewarm the butter sauce in the first skillet over medium heat. Transfer the cauliflower mixture into the butter and toss. Spoon the mixture over the scallops and serve immediately.

Zia Donata's Fava Bean Puree with Swiss Chard

If Puglia had to designate a regional vegetable, it would be fava beans. My mother's sister and my namesake, Donata, taught me how to cook with favas. The first step was to listen for the vegetable seller's 6 a.m. bullhorn call, which meant he was about to ride past the house on his donkey. I tasted favas prepared this way in the city of Lecce at Patria, a very beautiful, cosmopolitan restaurant, and it has become a favorite at Mia Dona. Make this only with dried favas; canned or frozen don't do it justice. If you find fresh favas, sprinkle a few steamed beans on top for color.

SERVES 4 TO 6

YOU'LL NEED:
immersion blender

1 pound small, dried, shelled fava beans

1 medium potato, peeled and coarsely chopped

½ carrot, peeled and coarsely chopped

1 small yellow onion, coarsely chopped

1 celery stalk with leaves, coarsely chopped

¼ cup extra-virgin olive oil plus more for drizzling

1 pound Swiss chard, tough stems removed (see Clean Greens, opposite page)

Kosher salt and freshly ground black pepper

8–12 slices rustic Italian bread

¼ cup Parmigiano-Reggiano shavings made with a vegetable peeler

PUT THE DRIED BEANS in a large saucepan with 6 cups of water. Bring to a gentle boil, then reduce the heat and simmer for about 25 minutes. As foam rises to the surface, skim it off with a spoon. Add the potato, carrot, onion, celery, and 2 tablespoons of olive oil, cover, and cook on low heat until the beans are tender, about 1 hour more. Add up to 1 cup of water to the beans if the liquid evaporates before the beans are cooked. Puree until smooth using an immersion blender.

HEAT THE REMAINING 2 TABLESPOONS of olive oil in a large skillet over high heat. Add the greens, reduce the heat, and sauté for a few minutes, until the greens are wilted. Season with salt and pepper.

MEANWHILE, BRUSH THE BREAD with olive oil. Using tongs, "grill" the bread slices on both sides over a gas flame or by placing the bread directly on the coils of an electric burner, taking care not to let it char.

TO SERVE, SPOON the puree into bowls. Top with a mound of greens and shaved Parmigiano. Serve warm with the grilled bread.

chef tip: clean greens

Just a single granule of dirt or grit left on greens can ruin a dish. Be sure to clean them thoroughly before using. To do this properly, fill the sink with water, gently submerge the greens, and let soak for 10 minutes. Lift the greens out of the water into a colander or salad spinner and drain the sink of the water and grit. Repeat until there is no grit resting on the bottom of the sink.

SPRING BUFFET

This buffet is perfect for a bridal or baby shower, Easter, Mother's Day—or as an excuse to celebrate the beginning of longer days.

SETTING THE SCENE

I LOVE NATURAL MATERIALS, and they just seem appropriate to use at this time of year, when we're all longing for the buds to come. Stone, marble, wood, slate, and glass mix beautifully with plain white pieces on the buffet table and can be used throughout the season. Rather than serve the frittata directly from the pan (which is perfectly lovely if the pan fits into the scheme of your setting), I cut it up and arrange the pieces on a wooden board (who says bread boards are only for bread?). Make it a point to bring the beauty of the season inside, as I do with a few budding branches. They lend more drama to the spread than do fussy bouquets. Depending on where you live, you can

WHAT TO SERVE

menu

BRESAOLA PURSES, page 23

CHERRY TOMATO, MINT, ASPARAGUS, AND GRUYÉRE FRITTATA, page 143

QUINOA, TABBOULEH-STYLE, page 185

TOMATO-CUCUMBER SALAD, page 64

LAMB CHOPS WITH LEMON-MINT GREMOLATA, page 148

SEARED AHI WITH WATERCRESS AND YOGURT SAUCE, page 149

ZIA DONATA'S RICOTTA CHEESECAKE, page 214

COTTON CANDY, page 222

literally snip a branch off a tree. If you don't have access to fresh branches, don't be afraid to fake it with silk buds. Because the buffet table is full, I let the vase and the salad bowl act as the only decoration.

WHAT TO POUR

MIMOSAS, BELLINIS, CHAMPAGNE, prosecco, kir royale—sooo elegant, sooo good! Done! Buy beautiful ribbon in your favorite color and tie it around the stems of your champagne glasses for added drama.

 ## WHAT TO PLAY

I'M NO DJ, so discovering www.pandora.com was a lifesaver for me—just select a few favorite songs in a genre you like and it will act as your DJ. A spring buffet is best suited to light easy rock—even a little Carly Simon, Maroon 5, and Joni Mitchell would work.

WHAT TO WEAR

GO FOR LIGHT COLORS in the spring, but you don't have to be an Easter egg—beautiful taupes and neutrals in flowing fabrics are wonderful. Flouncy mini skirts are fun as well! Keep your hair and makeup on the natural side for a daytime event and avoid obvious evening attire like sequins or satin.

chapter three *and* PASTA GRAINS

Winter

Donatella's Italian Mac and Cheese

Orecchiette with Broccoli Rabe

Mezze Rigate with Roasted Cauliflower and Bacon

Farotto with Kale, Speck, and Thyme

Spring

Gemelli Principessa

Lentils and Ditalini with Parsley-Mint Pesto

Tagliatelle with Fava Beans and Young Pecorino

Savoy Cabbage, Pancetta, and Red Onion Risotto

Summer

Donatella's Tearless Paella

Summer Lasagna

Cavatelli alla Crudiola

Crab Risotto with Salmon Caviar and Fresh Herbs

Fall

Saffron Risotto

Red Wine and Rosemary Risotto

Rita's Stuffed Shells

Papardelle with Black Truffles and Chives

Buckwheat Bucatini with Kale and Taleggio

Paccheri al Cardinale

I've been making and eating pasta ever since I can remember, at least as far back as 3 years old. I ate it every day growing up. Today, if you ask me what I'm going to make myself for dinner, 9 times out of 10 the answer is pasta. And while Italians typically eat pasta before the main course, I have no problem serving it to guests as the main course, especially if it is a hearty dish, which most inherently are. In fact, just about all of the recipes in this chapter will serve 4 as an entrée or 6 as a first course.

Never was pasta more celebrated in recent memory than in *Big Night*, the bittersweet story of two Italian brothers in search of the American dream. Sometime after the movie premiered, a friend was at a dinner party and happened to be seated next to Stanley Tucci, the actor who played one of the brothers. It inspired her to invite the city's food press to my home, where I prepared a Neapolitan dinner in the spirit of the film. Let me tell you, there's nothing like watching some of the country's top food journalists go limp with joy at the sight of a *timballo* (or *timpano*, as it was referred to in the movie), a molded pasta bound with cheese and baked. I felt like I was the most amazing cook in the room that night.

Before the crowd dug in, I served up antipasto platters of marinated mushrooms, artichokes, and buffalo ricotta, and afterward a beautiful, simple salad of radicchio, endive, and arugula lightly dressed with a lemon vinaigrette. All the while, the movie soundtrack streamed into the room. I chose red and white Neapolitan wines to go with each course and sent guests off at the end of the night with a tiny bottle of limoncello. After a course of cheeses, roasted chestnuts, and pear compote, I served a lemon tart along with Amaretti di Sarrono cookies, which meant that I could perform the flying-fire paper trick (see page 232). In the end, there was nothing more satisfying than sitting back in my chair, pleasantly full, watching guests do the same.

I have not included a recipe for timballo in this chapter (if you're going to spend a better part of a day cooking, I'd rather you make my Mama's Meatballs, page 141!) but there are plenty of other dishes, including Paccheri al Cardinale and Donatella's Tearless Paella that I guarantee will invoke an equally dramatic reaction from your guests. Even my Mac and Cheese gets a remarkable facelift from beaten egg whites.

Pasta brings people together, at least that was the message I got growing up. Even after late closings at his restaurant, my father would arrive home with a few friends and toss together a simple pasta dish for them. And that's the beauty of it. Depending on how you prepare it, pasta can star on a big night or on a casual evening with friends; it's all in what ingredients you add to it. The same is true for the rice and other grains and pulses, including quinoa, farro, and lentils featured on the following pages. If you master one dish in each season, you can entertain for life.

PASTA AND RISOTTO

do's and don'ts

Making pasta and risotto is second nature to me, and my hope is that by preparing dishes like Crab Risotto, Papardelle with Black Truffles, Cavatelli alla Crudiola, or Saffron Risotto, you will begin to improvise and decide for yourself what ingredients you want to toss into your pasta and rice.

As easy as the pasta dishes are, there are a few simple things you can do to make them foolproof. Pasta needs to move and dance around in its cooking water, so start with cold water, give it an ample supply, and make it salty. If you're not sure if the pasta is cooked *al dente*, just split open a piece. If there's a line down the middle, it needs to spend a little more time in the pot. Always, always, always (unless otherwise instructed in the recipe) marry the pasta to the sauce by removing it from the cooking water with a spider (a wire skimmer with a curved shape) or a large slotted spoon and tossing it in the pot with the sauce. Turn the heat to high and toss the pasta in the sauce for 30 seconds. Draining the pasta robs it of some of the starchy cooking water that helps to bring the sauce and pasta together.

TIPS FOR MAKING PERFECT RISOTTO

There are a few tips a cook should have up her sleeve when making risottos, too.

• Use a heavy-bottomed pot and wooden spoon to stir.

• Finely grate the cheese so that it melts quickly when added at the end of the cooking process, and cut the chilled butter added at the end into ½" pieces.

• Finely chop onions so that they cook through and don't affect the texture of the finished risotto. Do not let them burn when cooking in the butter and oil.

• To avoid making soupy risotto, reduce the amount of stock added toward the end; you can always stir in a little hot stock to loosen it up after you add the butter and cheese.

• Have all ingredients ready because you will be adding them continuously as the rice cooks.

Donatella's Italian Mac and Cheese

If I'm going to tweak a beloved classic like macaroni and cheese, the results had better be infinitely better than the tried and true. I swear on my Manolos that this version will not let you down. It's all about the cheese choices: I use top-quality Taleggio, pecorino, and Parmigiano for sharpness and tang, and creamy mascarpone for richness and texture. At the last minute, I decided to fold some whipped egg whites into it to make the whole thing lighter—tell your guests it's macaroni and cheese soufflé. I know what you're thinking: mac 'n' cheese for a dinner party? If you bake it in individual ramekins (portions spooned from a large casserole are not pretty!) and drizzle a little truffle oil on top, absolutely. (See photo page 88.)

SERVES 6 TO 8

YOU'LL NEED:
8-ounce ramekins

1 tablespoon plus 2 teaspoons kosher salt

1 pound imported elbow macaroni

3 large egg whites

½ cup (1 stick) unsalted butter plus more for greasing ramekins

½ medium onion, finely chopped

⅓ cup all-purpose flour

3½ cups whole milk

1 bay leaf

1 sprig fresh thyme

9 black peppercorns

Freshly ground black pepper

¼ teaspoon ground nutmeg

1 cup mascarpone

6 ounces Taleggio cheese, rind removed and diced

6 ounces Parmigiano-Reggiano, grated

6 ounces Pecorino Romano, coarsely grated

1 cup Garlic Bread Crumbs (recipe follows)

Truffle oil, for drizzling

BUTTER THE RAMEKINS. Preheat the oven to 375°F.

BRING A LARGE POT of water with 1 tablespoon of salt to a boil. Add the pasta and stir just until the water returns to a boil. Cook until just al dente, drain, shaking well. Meanwhile, beat the egg whites to stiff peaks.

MELT THE BUTTER in a large saucepan over medium-low heat. Add the onion and cook until softened. Sprinkle the flour over the onion and stir constantly for 2 minutes; don't allow the flour to brown. Add 1 cup of the milk a little at a time, stirring constantly. Stir until smooth, and then add the bay leaf, thyme, peppercorns, and the remaining 2 teaspoons of salt and 2½ cups of milk. Increase the heat to medium-high and continue stirring frequently until the liquid reaches a boil (don't let it boil over). Boil for 1 minute, then reduce the heat to low so the milk barely simmers, and continue to cook, stirring frequently, for 10 minutes more. Remove from the heat and let stand for 5 minutes, and then strain through a sieve into a very large bowl, working the onions back and forth with a rubber spatula to extract all the liquid possible. Immediately stir in plenty of ground pepper, the nutmeg, mascarpone, Tallegio, Parmigiano-Reggiano, and Pecorino Romano, stirring until the cheeses are just melted.

STIR THE COOKED MACARONI into the cheese mixture, then fold in the beaten egg whites. Spoon the mixture into the ramekins, mounding slightly, and top each with a big pinch of the bread crumbs.

BAKE FOR 25 TO 30 MINUTES, until the cheese is quietly sizzling and the bread crumbs are golden. Let cool for 5 minutes, drizzle with the truffle oil, and serve.

Garlic Bread Crumbs

MAKES 2 CUPS

5 ounces (about 3 thick slices), country-style white bread, crusts removed

2 large garlic cloves, minced or pushed through a garlic press

½ teaspoon salt

¼ teaspoon freshly ground black pepper

2½ tablespoons olive oil

PULSE THE BREAD in a food processor until it is in coarse crumbs.

TOSS THE CRUMBS with the garlic, salt, and pepper in a large mixing bowl until thoroughly combined. Add the olive oil and work vigorously with a rubber spatula to force the oil into the crumbs.

Orecchiette with Broccoli Rabe

I made this classic Apulian dish on my first appearance on the Martha Stewart show. I showed Martha how to make the orecchiette by hand, the way my aunts taught me. In their Puglian town of Toritto, it's not unusual to see trays of orecchiette set on stools outside the front door, drying in the sun. It's not necessary to make your own pasta, of course; I recommend De Cecco. If you're swearing off meat, leave out the sausage and instead add a teaspoon of anchovy paste when sautéing the olive oil.

SERVES 4 TO 6

1 pound broccoli rabe, tough ends trimmed, cut into 3" pieces

1 pound orecchiette

½ cup extra-virgin olive oil

1 pound sweet Italian sausage, casing removed and meat crumbled

3 garlic cloves, coarsely chopped

½ teaspoon red-pepper flakes

⅓ cup freshly grated Parmigiano-Reggiano

Kosher salt and freshly ground black pepper

BRING A LARGE POT of generously salted cold water to a boil. Add the broccoli rabe and cook 5 to 6 minutes, until tender (do not overcook). Remove the broccoli rabe to a colander with a slotted spoon and place under cold running water to stop the cooking.

RETURN THE WATER to a boil, add the pasta, and cook according to package directions until al dente. Meanwhile, heat 2 tablespoons of the olive oil in a large skillet over medium heat. Add the sausage and cook, breaking it up with a wooden spoon, until it loses all of its pink color. Transfer the sausage to a plate and set aside.

HEAT THE REMAINING 6 tablespoons of olive oil in the same skillet over medium heat. Add the broccoli rabe, garlic, and red-pepper flakes and cook, stirring, for 30 seconds. Return the sausage to the skillet and stir. When the pasta is ready, use a spider to lift it out of the water and add to the skillet, allowing the water drippings from the pasta to fall in. Add half the Parmigiano and season with salt and pepper. Raise the heat to high and toss for 30 seconds. Sprinkle the remaining Parmigiano onto the pasta and serve.

Mezze Rigate with Roasted Cauliflower and Bacon

This takes me straight to the dinner table of my childhood, where cauliflower was common and comforting. I serve it sprinkled with pecorino, but my mother occasionally spooned toasted bread crumbs on top, which I recall thinking was just about the best thing I ever tasted. To make it the way my mother did, sprinkle with Garlic Bread Crumbs (page 95). Adding the chicken stock to the roasting pan keeps the cauliflower moist.

SERVES 4 TO 6

1 small head cauliflower florets, trimmed into ¾" pieces

5 tablespoons extra-virgin olive oil

Kosher salt and freshly ground black pepper

¼ cup low-sodium chicken broth or water

6 ounces thick-cut bacon, cut into matchstick strips

6 garlic cloves, very finely chopped

¾ cup dry white wine

1 pound imported mezze penne rigate or garganelli

1½ cups grated pecorino cheese

⅓ cup roughly chopped flat-leaf parsley

PREHEAT THE OVEN to 500°F.

COMBINE THE CAULIFLOWER with 2 tablespoons of the olive oil in a baking dish and toss to coat. Season with salt and pepper, then drizzle all over with the chicken broth. Roast about 15 minutes, until golden and tender.

BRING A VERY LARGE POT of generously salted water to a boil. Cook the bacon in the remaining 3 tablespoons of olive oil in a heavy-bottomed pot until golden. Add the garlic and cook for 30 seconds more. Add the white wine, 1 teaspoon of salt, and plenty of pepper. Bring to a simmer, then remove from the heat.

COOK THE PASTA according to package directions until al dente. When the pasta is ready, use a spider to lift it out of the water and transfer to the bacon mixture, allowing the water drippings from the pasta to fall into the pot. Add the roasted cauliflower and enough of the reserved pasta water to make a light sauce. Raise the heat to high, toss well, add the pecorino and parsley and toss again. Serve warm.

Farotto with Kale, Speck, and Thyme

Farotto is a dish made with big nutty grains of farro (a type of wheat) cooked like risotto. In fact, you can substitute farro for the rice in any risotto dish, especially those that feature hearty or assertively flavored ingredients such as winter squash or bacon. Combined with kale and Italian speck, a smoky ham similar to prosciutto, it is the perfect winter dish. If you can't find speck (though you really should make it your business to do so), substitute pancetta or a smoked, low-sugar bacon. (See my Tips for Making Perfect Risotto, page 93, if this is a first for you.) Perfect served as an hors d'oeuvre in a spoon.

SERVES 4 TO 6

1½ cups farro

7 cups low-sodium chicken broth

2 tablespoons extra-virgin olive oil

1 small yellow onion, finely chopped

2 large sprigs fresh thyme

2 ounces speck, diced

½ cup dry white or red wine

Kosher salt

1 large bunch Tuscan, curly, or plain-leaved kale, stems removed and leaves washed and sliced crosswise into thin strips

Freshly ground black pepper

2 tablespoons extra-virgin olive oil or butter, for finishing (optional)

SOAK THE FARRO in water to cover for 1 hour and drain. Meanwhile, bring the chicken broth to a low simmer in a saucepan and partially cover.

WARM 2 TABLESPOONS OF THE OLIVE OIL in a large, heavy-bottomed pan over medium heat. Add the onion and thyme and stir until the onions are translucent and slightly golden. Add the speck and cook for 2 minutes more. Add the farro and stir to toast slightly, about 3 minutes. Add the wine and cook until it is completely absorbed. Add enough broth to cover the grains and 1 teaspoon of salt to the pot and stir constantly until the broth is absorbed. Continue adding enough broth to cover the grains, in batches, and stir, scraping down the sides. After about 14 minutes, stir in the kale leaves. Continue adding broth and stirring until it is absorbed and the farro is loose and creamy with a little bite at the center, about 14 minutes longer. Remove from the heat and season with salt and plenty of pepper. Remove the thyme sprigs. Stir in the 2 tablespoons olive oil or butter to finish, if desired. Serve hot.

Gemelli Principessa

Today, it may be as common as carrots, but at one time, only royalty ate asparagus—actually just the tender, meaty tip—thus the name of this dish. These days, you can find asparagus in the supermarket year round, but resist the urge to make this in any other season than spring, when the asparagus is at its sweetest and most abundant. If the guest list includes heartier eaters, sauté about 1 pound of sweet Italian sausage, breaking it up with a wooden spoon, before you add the pine nuts and the asparagus to the skillet.

SERVES 4 TO 6

1 tablespoon plus 1 teaspoon kosher salt

1 large bunch small or medium asparagus

1 pound imported gemelli or fusilli

2 tablespoons extra-virgin olive oil

½ cup pine nuts, toasted (see page 49)

⅓ cup heavy cream

1 cup sheep's milk ricotta (or best-quality fresh whole-milk ricotta)

Freshly ground black pepper

⅓ cup grated Parmigiano-Reggiano

20 large fresh basil leaves, torn into pieces

BRING A VERY LARGE POT of water to a boil and add 1 tablespoon of the salt. Cut 2" off the tips of the asparagus (reserve the asparagus ends for another use). Blanch the asparagus tips in the boiling water for 3 to 4 minutes (depending on their size) until just tender. Transfer to a colander using a large skimmer or spider and run under cold running water to stop the cooking.

BRING THE ASPARAGUS cooking water back to a boil. Add the pasta and cook according to package directions, until al dente. Meanwhile, heat the olive oil in a large skillet over medium heat. When it is warm, add all but about 1 tablespoon of the toasted pine nuts, the asparagus tips, the remaining teaspoon of salt, and the cream and simmer for about 2 minutes. When the pasta is just about cooked, use a large skimmer or spider to transfer it to the sauté pan. Add the ricotta, plenty of pepper, and about ½ cup of the pasta cooking water. Raise the heat to high, and toss until all the noodles are well coated, about 30 seconds. Add the Parmigiano and half the basil, and toss again. Transfer to a large platter, garnish with the reserved tablespoon of pine nuts and remaining basil, and serve.

Lentils and Ditalini with Parsley-Mint Pesto

Every Italian toddler knows ditalini, thimble-size pasta tubes that fit perfectly in little mouths and onto tiny fingertips. It is a shape beautifully suited to tiny French lentils, too, in this refreshing combination, perfect for lunch or a light dinner.

SERVES 4 TO 6

YOU'LL NEED:
Microplane zester

Pesto

2 garlic cloves, thinly sliced

2 shallots, thinly sliced

1 tablespoon pine nuts

¼ cup flat-leaf parsley

¼ cup mint leaves

¾ teaspoon kosher salt

Freshly ground black pepper

⅓ cup extra-virgin olive oil

1 teaspoon fresh lemon juice

Lentils and Ditalini

1 tablespoon olive oil

1 celery rib, finely chopped

¾ cup small French green lentils

1½ cups low-sodium chicken broth plus more if needed

¾ cup ditalini or orzo pasta

½ cup frozen peas, thawed

2 scallions, sliced ½" thick on a diagonal

Zest of 1 lemon

Kosher salt and freshly ground black pepper

TO MAKE THE PESTO: Combine the garlic, shallots, pine nuts, parsley, mint, salt, plenty of pepper, and olive oil in a small food processor. Blend until smooth. Cover and refrigerate until ready to serve. Stir in the lemon juice just before serving.

TO MAKE THE LENTILS: Heat the oil over medium-low heat in a large, heavy-bottomed saucepan. Add the celery and sauté until tender. Add the lentils and stir to coat them with oil. Add the broth; the lentils should be covered by liquid. Bring to a boil, then reduce the heat, partially cover the pan, and simmer gently for 25 to 30 minutes, until the lentils are tender but firm. Drain if necessary and let stand, uncovered, for 5 minutes.

MEANWHILE, BRING A MEDIUM POT of generously salted water to a boil. Add the pasta and cook according to package directions until al dente. One minute before the pasta is done, stir in the peas. When the pasta is ready, use a spider to lift the pasta and peas out of the water and add to the lentils, allowing the water drippings from the pasta to fall into the pan. Stir in the pesto, scallions, and lemon zest. Season to taste with salt and pepper. Serve warm or at room temperature.

Tagliatelle with Fava Beans and Young Pecorino

Peeling fava beans takes a little time, but the fresh and earthy flavor of this prized spring bean is well worth it. Paired with sheep's cheese, this combination screams spring in Italy. Use your well-manicured thumbnail to nick the opaque white skin surrounding the luminous green beans, then peel off the encasing skins with ease. Serve the pasta in a neat little beehive by twirling it onto a carving fork (page 120).

SERVES 4 TO 6

2 pounds fava beans in their pods

3 garlic cloves

¾ teaspoon kosher salt

⅔ cup firmly packed basil leaves

½ cup extra-virgin olive oil

1 pound dried imported tagliatelle

6 ounces soft, young pecorino cheese, such as Pientino, coarsely grated

4 ounces best-quality salted butter, cut into 8 pieces

Freshly ground black pepper

REMOVE THE FAVA BEANS from their pods. Bring a large pot of lightly salted water to a boil. Add the beans and cook for 2 minutes. Drain, rinse under cold water, and remove the white skins. This may be done the night before or a few hours ahead of time.

PULSE THE GARLIC in a food processor until finely chopped. Add about two-thirds of the peeled fava beans, the salt, basil, and olive oil. Pulse until roughly chopped, not perfectly smooth. Transfer to a large bowl.

BRING A VERY LARGE POT of generously salted water to a boil. Cook the tagliatelle according to package instructions until al dente. When the pasta is ready, use a spider to lift it out of the water and transfer it to the bowl of fava puree, allowing the water drippings from the pasta to fall into it. Add about ½ cup of the cooking water, the remaining whole fava beans, pecorino, and butter to the bowl and toss until the butter has only just melted and all the ingredients are evenly distributed. Season with plenty of pepper and serve warm.

chef tip: fresh or dried?

Just say no to fresh supermarket pasta. It may seem like the superior choice, but as a rule, dried tagliatelle, fettucini, and other shaped pastas are better, unless of course you make them yourself. De Cecco, a supermarket brand, is a favorite, as is Setaro, which is available in gourmet food shops.

Savoy Cabbage, Pancetta, and Red Onion Risotto

I love the combination of cabbage and onions—add creamy rice to the mix and it's even better. This is as formal as comfort food should get—a perfect dish to serve when you want to keep it casual, but not too much so. Vegetarians, use vegetable stock, skip the pancetta, and use smoked mozzarella to replace its smoky flavor.

SERVES 4 TO 6

4 ounces thick-sliced pancetta or smoked bacon, cut into matchstick strips

2 tablespoons extra-virgin olive oil

2 garlic cloves, smashed and sliced

1 small head Savoy cabbage, quartered, cored, and very thinly sliced

Kosher salt and freshly ground black pepper

2 tablespoons unsalted butter

1 red onion, finely chopped

6 cups low-sodium chicken broth

2 cups arborio or Carnaroli rice

½ cup white wine or vermouth

1½ cups grated Parmigiano-Reggiano, Pecorino Romano, or Grana Padano

4 ounces fresh mozzarella, cut into small chunks (optional)

COOK THE PANCETTA in 1 tablespoon of the olive oil in a large skillet over medium heat until the fat begins to render. Add the garlic and sauté about 1 minute, until soft and just golden. Stir in the cabbage and cover the pan. Steam for 5 minutes, then season lightly with salt and generously with pepper. Remove from the heat.

WARM THE REMAINING 1 TABLESPOON of olive oil and the butter in a large, heavy saucepan over medium-low heat. Add the onion and cook until softened but not browned. Meanwhile, bring the broth to a lower simmer in a saucepan. Partially cover and keep hot. Add the rice to the onions and stir constantly for 2 to 3 minutes, until the rice looks translucent. Add ½ teaspoon of salt and the wine and cook until it is absorbed. Add 1 cup of the hot stock, stirring constantly, until it is absorbed. Continue adding the stock 1 cup at a time, stirring constantly, until it is absorbed and the rice is creamy and slightly al dente, about 18 minutes. Stir in the pancetta and cabbage mixture, 1 cup of the Parmigiano and, if desired, the fresh mozzarella. Season with salt and pepper and serve warm with the remaining Parmigiano on the side.

Donatella's Tearless Paella

I fell in love with paella after traveling in Spain, but making it the traditional way is not easy. I've come up with a simplified method and a streamlined ingredient list (skip the traditional mussels and go heavy on the shrimp and scallops) so you won't be reduced to tears. If you can, use a paella pan so that you can serve it straight from the oven—the drama factor will skyrocket—but whatever pan you use, make sure it is no smaller than 12". Ask the fishmonger to devein the shrimp through the back of the shell, keeping the shell on.

SERVES 4 TO 6

Seafood

6 ounces shell-on shrimp, preferably deveined through the back of the shell

6 ounces bay scallops

3 garlic cloves, thickly sliced

2 tablespoons extra-virgin olive oil

1 tablespoon finely chopped flat-leaf parsley

Kosher salt and freshly ground black pepper

Cayenne pepper

1 tablespoon dry white wine or vermouth

2 teaspoons fresh lemon juice

Rice

2 cups low-sodium chicken broth

2 cups seafood or fish stock

2 tablespoons extra-virgin olive oil

4 ounces smoked bacon, cut into matchstick strips

1 Spanish onion, finely chopped

3 garlic cloves, very finely chopped

1 teaspoon saffron threads

2 cups Spanish bomba or vialone rice

1 teaspoon kosher salt

Freshly ground black pepper

4 ounces cured chorizo, thickly sliced

1 (10-ounce) package frozen artichokes, thawed

2 roasted red peppers (from a jar), cut into strips

2 scallions, thinly sliced

2 lemons, cut into wedges

TO MAKE THE SEAFOOD: Combine the shrimp, scallops, garlic, olive oil, parsley, a pinch of salt, plenty of pepper, a little dash of cayenne, the wine, and lemon juice in a bowl and toss. Cover and refrigerate at least 20 minutes and up to 2 hours.

MEANWHILE, PLACE A RACK in the lower third of the oven and preheat it to 350°F.

TO MAKE THE RICE: Combine the chicken broth and seafood stock in a saucepan and bring to a simmer. In a 12" ovenproof skillet or sauté pan, heat the olive oil over medium heat. Add the bacon and sauté until golden brown. Transfer to a plate using a slotted spoon. Add the onion to the pan and sauté until softened, about 5 minutes. Add the garlic and saffron and cook about 2 minutes, until the garlic is fragrant and soft. Add the rice and stir about 3 minutes, until it's slightly translucent. Season with salt and plenty of pepper. Add the hot broth. Simmer, uncovered, for about 4 minutes, to allow it to reduce slightly, then cover the pan with a lid or aluminum foil and transfer to the oven.

BAKE THE RICE MIXTURE for 30 minutes. Discard the garlic slices from the shrimp and scallops. Increase the oven temperature to 450°F. Remove the pan from the oven and nestle the chorizo and artichokes into the rice without stirring it. Sprinkle the bacon and the roasted peppers on top, then spoon the shrimp and scallops attractively over all, drizzling with a little of their marinade. Re-cover the pan and bake for 8 minutes more. Remove the cover, garnish with the scallions and lemon wedges, and serve directly from the pan.

donatella clicks

Whenever I serve this paella, I tend to stick to a Spanish theme, foodwise. La Tienda (www.latienda.com) is a gold mine of fine-quality paella ingredients (rice, bouillon tablets, sweet smoked paprika, saffron) as well as authentic paella pans, Spanish wines, and dozens of tapas.

Summer Lasagna

Italians picnic on lasagna the way Americans do fried chicken! My mother always made this in a foil pan the day before we went to the beach, allowing the flavors to improve overnight. It holds up beautifully when cut in squares and, of course, is ideal for transporting.

SERVES 6 TO 8

Vegetarian Bolognese

½ cup extra-virgin olive oil

1 medium onion, grated

2 celery stalks, grated

1 medium carrot, peeled and grated

3 large zucchini, trimmed and grated

3 cups button mushrooms, coarsely chopped

2 garlic cloves, smashed and coarsely chopped

1 sprig fresh rosemary

Pinch of red-pepper flakes

Salt and freshly ground black pepper

1 (28-ounce) can Italian tomatoes

Lasagna

1 pound fresh ricotta

2 large egg yolks

¾ cup grated Parmigiano-Reggiano or Grana Padano

1¼ cups grated smoked mozzarella

1 large shallot, finely chopped

1 tablespoon dry white wine or vermouth

2 tablespoons roughly chopped flat-leaf parsley

1 tablespoon + 1 teaspoon kosher salt

Freshly ground black pepper

1 (18-ounce) package lasagna noodles (12 sheets)

1 tablespoon pine nuts, toasted (page 49) and chopped

¼ cup Garlic Bread Crumbs (page 95)

4 basil leaves, cut into chiffonade

TO MAKE THE VEGETARIAN BOLOGNESE: Heat the oil in a large saucepan over medium-high heat. Add the grated onion, celery, carrot, zucchini, mushrooms, garlic, rosemary, and red-pepper flakes. Cook, stirring often, until the vegetables release their moisture and begin to soften, about 8 to 10 minutes. Season well with salt and pepper.

DRAIN THE TOMATOES, reserving the juices, and use your hands to crush the tomatoes directly into the pot. Add the reserved tomato juices and stir.

REDUCE THE HEAT to a simmer and cook until the sauce is thickened, about 15 minutes. Season again with salt and pepper.

COAT A 9" × 12" BAKING DISH with olive oil. Preheat the oven to 350°F. Combine the ricotta, egg yolks, ½ cup of the Parmigiano, mozzarella, shallot, wine, parsley, 1 teaspoon salt, and plenty of pepper in a bowl.

BOIL THE LASAGNA NOODLES in plenty of salted water until just before al dente (these will continue to cook when baked in the oven). Arrange 3 sheets of lasagna on the bottom of the dish. Spread one-quarter of the ricotta mixture over them. Spoon about one-third of the vegetable bolognese mixture on top. Repeat this twice more, making sure there are no exposed noodle edges that are not covered with ricotta. Top the last layer of lasagna noodles with the last quarter of the ricotta. Combine the pine nuts, bread crumbs, and remaining ¼ cup of Parmigiano in a small bowl. Sprinkle evenly over the ricotta. Cover with foil and bake for 30 minutes. Remove the foil, raise the heat to 450°F, and bake 8 to 10 minutes more, until golden. Let stand for 10 to 15 minutes. Garnish with the fresh basil, cut into squares, and serve.

Cavatelli alla Crudiola

If this pasta were any easier, friends might come away thinking you're a culinary lightweight. Admittedly, a grade-schooler could make the no-cook sauce, but your genius lies in bringing the pasta and sauce together. The secret is to add half of the cheese to the hot pasta just before you toss it with the sauce. This helps unite the two beautifully. Using the freshest ingredients, including top-quality olive oil and salt, is key here. Gaeta olives are a personal favorite, but capers are also nice.

SERVES 4 TO 6

YOU'LL NEED:
box grater

1 pint pear or cherry tomatoes, halved lengthwise

½ cup Gaeta olives, pitted and roughly chopped

3 large garlic cloves, peeled and lightly crushed

30 small baby green and purple basil leaves plus a few sprigs for garnish

¼ cup extra-virgin olive oil

Kosher salt and freshly ground black pepper

1 pound cavatelli

5 ounces ricotta salata, shredded on the large holes of a box grater

COMBINE THE TOMATOES, olives, garlic, basil, and olive oil in a large serving bowl. Season with salt and pepper. Toss to coat the tomatoes evenly and set aside at room temperature.

BRING A LARGE POT of generously salted water to a boil. Cook the pasta according to package directions until al dente. Remove the garlic cloves from the tomato mixture, and, using a spider or slotted spoon, transfer the pasta to the serving bowl, allowing the pasta water drippings to fall in. Add half of the cheese and ¼ cup of the pasta water and toss. Season to taste with salt and pepper. Sprinkle the remaining cheese on top and garnish with basil. Serve warm or at room temperature.

chef tip: pasta the next day

My mother's fried pasta is one of my fondest childhood food memories. She would dump any leftovers into a frying pan slicked with hot, hot olive oil and fry it until most of the pasta pieces were crisp and darkened, then sprinkle a little salt and pepper and dried oregano on top. I loooooved it, especially if the pasta happened to be ziti, but cavatelli will crisp up just as nicely. Another favorite? She would mix leftover pasta into a mixture of eggs, cheese, parsley, and salt and pepper and cook it as you would an omelet.

Crab Risotto with Salmon Caviar and Fresh Herbs

When I was a little girl, my dad taught me how to make risotto with truffles one Sunday. I remember standing next to him holding a wooden spoon as I stirred and he poured the broth. I love the combination of crabmeat and salmon caviar; it feels expensive, but it's not.

SERVES 4 TO 6 AS A FIRST COURSE

7 cups seafood stock or vegetable stock

2 tablespoons unsalted butter

1 tablespoon olive oil

2 large shallots, finely chopped

1 small celery heart, finely chopped (optional)

1 tablespoon tomato paste

1¼ cups white wine

2¼ cups arborio or Carnaroli rice

Kosher salt and freshly ground black pepper

8 ounces lump crabmeat

Small handful tiny sprigs fresh dill or chervil, or snipped chives

½–¾ cup crème fraîche (optional)

2 ounces salmon caviar

BRING THE STOCK TO A SIMMER in a saucepan. Partially cover and keep hot.

WARM THE BUTTER and oil in a large, heavy-bottomed pot. Add the shallots and celery, if using, and sauté until tender, about 5 minutes. Stir in the tomato paste and cook for 1 minute. Add the wine and simmer, uncovered, until it has completely evaporated. Add the rice, 1 teaspoon each of salt and pepper, and stir for 2 to 3 minutes, until the kernels begin to turn opaque. Add enough hot stock to cover the rice and stir until it is almost completely absorbed. Continue adding enough stock just to cover the rice, in batches, stirring and scraping down the sides of the pan until the risotto is loose and creamy, about 18 to 20 minutes. Stir in the crabmeat, breaking it up, then remove from the heat. Stir in the dill and season to taste with salt and pepper.

TOP EACH SERVING with a dollop of crème fraîche and a spoonful of salmon caviar.

Saffron Risotto

I'm not one to fool with perfection, but this time-honored Milanese classic was just begging for a little bling. Nothing short of gold is worthy to keep company with the saffron, the most expensive spice in the world, and where there's edible gold, there's glamour. In fact, for centuries, gold dust has been used to decorate food, prized for not only its beauty but for its symbolic power and alleged, yes, magical properties. Whatever its powers, shower a little on this delicious rice; purists will hardly disapprove.

SERVES 4 TO 6

6 cups homemade or low-sodium chicken stock or broth

½ teaspoon roughly chopped saffron threads

3 tablespoons unsalted butter

2 tablespoons olive oil

1 medium onion, very finely chopped

2 cups arborio or Carnaroli rice

½ cup dry white wine

Kosher salt and freshly ground black pepper

½ cup grated Parmigiano-Reggiano, plus extra for serving

Edible gold leaf (see below)

Very tender small sprigs of fresh lemon thyme, preferably with flowers, for garnish

BRING THE STOCK TO A SIMMER in a saucepan. Partially cover and keep warm. Soak the saffron threads in 1 cup of warm stock for 20 minutes.

COMBINE 1 TABLESPOON of the butter, the olive oil, and the onion in a large, heavy-bottomed saucepan over medium-high heat. Cook, stirring for about 5 minutes, until the onion is translucent. Add the rice, and stir to coat each grain with oil and butter. Add the wine and simmer until completely evaporated. Add ½ cup of hot stock, and continue stirring until almost all of the liquid has been absorbed into the rice. Continue adding the stock, ½ cup at a time, stirring until it is absorbed. Add the saffron-infused stock after about 10 minutes and cook, stirring for 8 or 9 minutes more; the rice should be firm to the bite and the mixture creamy. Remove from the heat and stir in the remaining 2 tablespoons of butter, salt, plenty of pepper, and ½ cup of the Parmigiano. Transfer to serving dishes, lay gold leaf in the center, garnish with the thyme, and serve with the grated Parmigiano on the side.

donatella clicks

 Kerekes baking supply company's online catalog (www.bakedeco.com) offers an assortment of edible golds and silvers larger than the selection at your average jewelry store.

Red Wine and Rosemary Risotto

Wine really is the star in this gorgeous rose-tinted risotto, so it's important to use a fairly good one. Because fontina is made in Italy's Piedmont region, I typically use a wine made from Nebbiolo grapes, the varietal used to make the pricey Barolos from that same area.

SERVES 4 TO 6

3½ cups chicken or vegetable stock

2 tablespoons unsalted butter

1 tablespoon extra-virgin olive oil

1 white or yellow onion, finely chopped

4 garlic cloves, finely chopped

1½ teaspoons finely chopped fresh rosemary

2¼ cups arborio or Carnaroli rice

1 teaspoon kosher salt plus more to taste

2 cups dry red wine, such as a Barolo

5 ounces fontina cheese, cut into small chunks

¼ cup roughly chopped baby arugula leaves

Freshly ground black pepper

BRING THE STOCK TO A SIMMER in a saucepan. Partially cover and keep warm.

WARM THE BUTTER and olive oil in a large, heavy-bottomed saucepan over medium-low heat. Add the onion and cook about 1 minute, until softened but not browned. Add the garlic and rosemary and cook for 30 seconds. Add the rice and stir until the rice looks slightly opaque, 2 to 3 minutes. Add 1 teaspoon salt and the red wine and cook until the wine is absorbed. Add enough stock to cover the grains and cook, stirring, until it is absorbed. Continue adding enough stock to cover the grains, stirring after each addition, until the rice is creamy and slightly al dente, about 18 minutes. Stir in the fontina and arugula and remove the pan from the heat. Season with salt and pepper and serve.

Rita's Stuffed Shells

Stuffed shells is one of those old-school recipes that everyone loves because it is just so good. I love it because it is incredibly easy to prepare, yet my guests think I slaved in the kitchen. This recipe comes from my good friend Rita, who has shared her incredible Neapolitan dishes with a great many chefs.

SERVES 6 TO 9

1 pound jumbo pasta shells (approximately 24–36 shells)

3 tablespoons extra-virgin olive oil

1½ pounds lean ground beef

2 garlic cloves, peeled and crushed

1½ teaspoons salt

½ teaspoon freshly ground black pepper

1 (28-ounce) can peeled Italian tomatoes

1 (15-ounce) container whole milk ricotta cheese

1⅓ cups grated Parmigiano-Reggiano

LIGHTLY OIL A 12" × 9" × 2" BAKING DISH and a rimmed baking sheet. Bring a large pot of salted water to a boil.

ADD THE PASTA SHELLS to the boiling water and cook just until slightly tender, 4 to 6 minutes; they should still be quite firm to the bite. Drain the pasta shells and arrange them on the oiled baking sheet, spreading them out so that they don't stick together.

HEAT 1 TABLESPOON OF THE OLIVE OIL in a large skillet and, when hot, add the ground beef and 1 crushed garlic clove. Season with salt and pepper and cook, stirring, until cooked through and no longer pink, 6 to 8 minutes. Transfer to a medium mixing bowl and set aside to cool slightly.

IN ANOTHER SKILLET, heat the remaining 2 tablespoons of olive oil. Add the remaining garlic and the tomatoes with their juices. Season with salt and pepper, bring the sauce to a simmer, and cook over low heat for at least 15 minutes, or until somewhat thickened.

STIR 1½ CUPS of the tomato sauce into the cooled ground beef, then add the ricotta and ⅔ cup of the Parmigiano and combine thoroughly. Preheat the oven to 350°F.

SPOON 1¼ CUPS of the tomato sauce into the prepared baking dish. Fill each pasta shell with some of the meat and cheese mixture, about 2 tablespoons per shell. Arrange the shells in the prepared baking dish. Spoon the remaining sauce over the shells and sprinkle with the remaining ⅔ cup of Parmigiano.

BAKE THE SHELLS until the filling is heated through and the top is golden brown.

Papardelle with Black Truffles and Chives

Unlike winter truffles—which will set you back big time—summer truffles cost about the same as a decent bottle of wine. Their flavor is subtle, but still "truffly." Don't shave the truffle until just before you cook the pasta, or some of its aroma will be lost. Serve this as a first course—it's too rich to eat a large portion—on plates warmed in a low oven. And if truffles, cream, and butter aren't decadent enough, drizzle a little truffle oil over each serving.

SERVES 6

1 black summer truffle, about the size of a golf ball

4 ounces best-quality butter, such as Plugrá

¼ cup heavy cream

Kosher salt and freshly ground black pepper

1 pound papardelle pasta

3 tablespoons snipped chives

RINSE THE TRUFFLE and use a sharp vegetable peeler to shave it, peel and all, into paper-thin slices. Set aside.

BRING A VERY LARGE POT of generously salted water to a boil. Meanwhile, bring the butter and cream to a simmer in a large skillet or sauté pan and season with ½ teaspoon salt and plenty of pepper. Cook the pasta in the boiling water according to package directions until al dente. When the pasta is ready, use a spider or skimmer to lift it out of the water and transfer to the skillet, allowing the water drippings from the pasta to fall in. Add half the chives and toss with tongs to coat the noodles evenly. Serve in warm bowls, garnished with the remaining chives and the truffle slices.

the girl can twirl

My dad's first job in America was as a waiter in an Italian restaurant where pasta was served tableside. Twirling pasta into a beautiful nest became second nature to him and, after a few tries, to me as well. It requires nothing more than a large two-pronged carving fork and a little twirling: Put the fork into the pasta and twirl until the fork can't handle anymore. Slide the pasta off the fork onto the center of the plate for a beautiful presentation.

Buckwheat Bucatini with Kale and Taleggio

Italians obviously have no fear of carbs—we eat pasta and potatoes together whenever the occasion calls for something hearty. This recipe is a great one for a casual Friday evening get-together. As for the carbohydrates, look at it this way: Buckwheat bucatini is not only friendly to your gluten-intolerant friends, but it is ridiculously healthful—full of fiber, protein, and magnesium. If you can't find artisanal buckwheat pasta, substitute whole-wheat bucatini, fettuccine, or tagliatelle.

Keeping the Taleggio cheese cold makes it easier to grate. If you choose not to use the anchovies, increase the salt to ¾ teaspoon.

SERVES 4 TO 6

1 bunch kale, stems removed

1 pound buckwheat bucatini or whole-wheat fettuccine or tagliatelle

6 large red-skinned potatoes, washed, peeled, and sliced ¼" thick

2 tablespoons extra-virgin olive oil

6 garlic cloves, thinly sliced

2 oil-packed anchovy fillets or 1 teaspoon anchovy paste (optional)

¼–½ teaspoon red-pepper flakes

Kosher salt and freshly ground black pepper

Pinch of ground nutmeg

6 ounces Taleggio or fontina cheese

¼ cup grated Parmigiano-Reggiano (optional)

BRING A VERY LARGE POT of generously salted water to a boil. Add the kale and cook for 3 minutes. Transfer the kale to a colander using a slotted spoon, and rinse under cold running water. Squeeze dry and coarsely chop. Add the bucatini to the boiling water, cook for 3 minutes, then add the potatoes to the same pot. Cook about 7 minutes more, until the pasta is still firm and chewy.

MEANWHILE, HEAT THE OLIVE OIL in a large skillet over medium-high heat. Add the garlic, anchovies (if using), and red-pepper flakes. Sauté, stirring, about 2 minutes, until the garlic is soft and fragrant. Add the kale and cook, stirring once or twice, for 2 to 3 minutes.

TRANSFER THE BUCATINI and potatoes to the skillet using a large spider or skimmer. Add ½ cup of the cooking water, ½ teaspoon salt, plenty of pepper, and the nutmeg. Toss to blend, then scatter the Taleggio and Parmigiano (if using) over the pasta, cover the pan, and remove from the heat. Let stand for 1 minute to allow the cheese to melt slightly. Serve warm.

Paccheri al Cardinale

In Italy, cardinals eat better than anyone, including kings, and this dish is ideal when you want to bring a little drama to the table. At Mia Dona, we bake it to order in an earthenware crock covered in parchment paper. The server slashes the parchment open at the table and spoons a white cloud of fresh ricotta on top.

SERVES 4 TO 6

YOU'LL NEED: parchment paper

Tomato Sauce

¾ cup olive oil

8 garlic cloves, chopped

1 (28-ounce) can crushed tomatoes

Kosher salt and freshly ground black pepper

Paccheri

1 pound paccheri or rigatoni

½ cup grated pecorino

½ cup grated Parmigiano-Reggiano

½ cup grated smoked mozzarella

20 basil leaves, cut into slivers

Kosher salt and freshly ground black pepper

1 cup fresh ricotta

TO MAKE THE TOMATO SAUCE: Heat the olive oil in a large pot over medium heat until hot but not smoking. Add the garlic and sauté about 2 minutes. Add the tomatoes and cook, stirring, for 5 minutes. Season with salt and pepper. Reduce the heat to low and simmer, partially covered, about 30 minutes, until thick.

TO MAKE THE PACCHERI: Preheat the oven to 450°F. Bring a large pot of generously salted water to a boil. Add the paccheri and cook until not quite al dente.

ADD THE PECORINO, Parmigiano, and mozzarella to the thickened tomato sauce and stir until the mozzarella melts. Stir in the basil. Season to taste with salt and pepper. Use a spider to lift the paccheri out of the water and into the sauce. Toss to coat, then transfer to a 4-quart casserole. Cover with parchment paper, tucking it into the sides of the dish. Bake about 20 minutes, until the pasta is piping hot. Bring the dish to the table, cut an "X" in the parchment, and gently tear back the points. Spoon some ricotta onto each portion.

donatella clicks

I prefer the Setaro brand of paccheri. Both it and the smoked mozzarella are available www.buonitalia.com.

CASUAL
SUMMER
DINNER

Summer is all about casual entertaining and simply by virtue of taking the party outside, you've created a laid-back vibe.

SETTING THE SCENE

NATURE PROVIDES THE DÉCOR so that you can focus on the table. Color is key—one of my favorites is turquoise, so I played it up through the napkins, the runner and some of the platters. It's always a nice idea to establish a one-color palette, or your table can end up looking like a box of Crayola

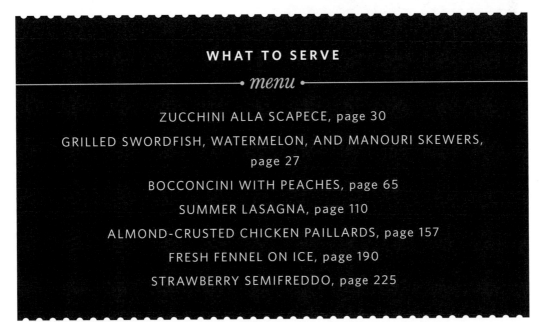

WHAT TO SERVE

• *menu* •

ZUCCHINI ALLA SCAPECE, page 30

GRILLED SWORDFISH, WATERMELON, AND MANOURI SKEWERS,
page 27

BOCCONCINI WITH PEACHES, page 65

SUMMER LASAGNA, page 110

ALMOND-CRUSTED CHICKEN PAILLARDS, page 157

FRESH FENNEL ON ICE, page 190

STRAWBERRY SEMIFREDDO, page 225

crayons (which has its place, but not on your table). Platters are also essential; not only do they eliminate multiple trips between the kitchen and the outdoor table, but they let the food do all of the talking. Use a mix of shapes and sizes to vary the pattern on the table. Rather than using linen, I chose an outdoor table runner from Chilewich (www. chilewich.com), whose product line I love, because of the easy cleanup. To give the table some height, I put the chilled fennel in a stately glass trifle bowl.

WHAT TO POUR

BEER AND WINE ARE CLASSICS for casual summer entertaining, but don't stop there. Pick an interesting selection of beer and keep it on ice. Grab a great but inexpensive red and white wine, and pour them into glass pitchers. Add some fresh apple or peach wedges to the pitchers and you have the perfect summer drink. Don't forget a nonalcoholic selection as well; sparkling water with lemon and lime wedges should do the trick.

WHAT TO PLAY

Think fun, upbeat, slightly retro:
CRUEL SUMMER-Bananarama
RIO by Duran Duran
Anything by the Beach Boys
PULLING MUSSELS FROM THE SHELL-Squeeze
BOYS OF SUMMER Don Henley

WHAT TO WEAR

SUMMER IS ALL ABOUT CASUAL, but that doesn't mean shorts and flip-flops. Jeans are fine, but dress them up with pretty heels and a flowy top. Maxi dresses are sexy and comfortable, and a great cocktail ring makes a statement without being fussy. Stay away from black for outdoor parties.

chapter four MAIN
COURSES

Winter

Pollo alla Contadini

Filet Mignon with Gorgonzola Sauce

Scampi Ribelli (Rebellious Shrimp)

Tilapia Oreganata

Mama's Meatballs

Spring

Cherry Tomato, Mint, Asparagus, and Gruyère Frittata

Robiola Pizza

Yellowtail alla Plancha

Lamb Chops with Lemon-Mint Gremolata

Seared Ahi with Watercress and Yogurt Sauce

Summer

Straccetti (Little Rags)

Veal Scallops with Eggplant and Melting Mozzarella

Grilled Whole Branzino with Sizzling Hazelnut Butter

Salmon in Cartoccio with Caponata

Almond-Crusted Chicken Paillards

Fall

Family-Style Polenta with Bolognese

Halibut in Phyllo with Porcini, Spinach, and Feta

Roasted Rack of Pork with Cabbage and Bacon

Steak Pizzaiola

The holidays made me do it! For years, I relied on tried-and-true pasta dishes to get me through the main course of a dinner party. They invariably came out fabulous and made me look the same. But when I realized that I had become the default host for the big family celebrations—including both Christmas and Easter—I knew it was time to change my ways and add some real main course entrées to my repertoire. But how could I compete with my mother's perfect meatballs and pork roast? My dad's Steak Pizzaiola? Zia Donata's Tilapia Oreganata? It seemed almost sacrilegious to even try to rival them.

I went back to my mother's house and cooked alongside her and spent time in relatives' and friends' kitchens in Italy, gleaning the tips, tricks, and secrets of making things like a lusty farmer's chicken, perfect polenta with Bolognese, and a fluffy frittata. Then I drew on my many years in the company of some of the country's top chefs. What I developed is a roster of recipes infused with the heart and soul of an Italian cook living a modern American life. I gave the beloved chicken cutlet of my youth a sophisticated makeover, coating it in a mixture of crushed almonds and featherweight panko crumbs. Cornish hens replaced the cut-up bird in my mother's hunter's chicken; they're just as succulent but present more beautifully on the plate. And I've deconstructed the classic (and too often poorly executed) veal Parmesan, stacking the essential ingredients—veal paillard, eggplant, mozzarella, and a little tomato sauce—one atop the other.

I find that in many restaurants, the appetizers and first courses are infinitely more interesting than the main courses. My theory is that chefs find they get to exercise a lot more creativity with the smaller plates; they have more room to experiment. When it comes to the entrées, playing it safe seems to rule the day. I've made sure that the recipes that follow are forgiving, but that doesn't mean they're any less alluring than their smaller counterparts. Wrapping fish in parchment is smart and sexy. The paper seals in juices *and* makes for a provocative presentation. And how better to flaunt your culinary prowess than to arrive at the table with a whole grilled fish on a platter?

When it comes to cooking meat, I keep it simple—and rely on my butcher to do much of the preparation. A roast rack of pork is one of the easiest entrées you can make, especially if you have the butcher remove the rack and tie it back on so there's no struggle when it's time to slice it into chops. The dish called straccetti is just thin slices of beef tossed quickly in hot oil—there is truly nothing more to it and the results are to die for. My father's Steak Pizzaiola is here, too—I finally got up the nerve to make it—with his secrets for cooking it just right.

There's only one recipe in this chapter that may not seem very glamorous to be prepared, but you only have to make Mama's Meatballs once—preferably on a leisurely Sunday—to convince you that a day spent in the kitchen can be as meditative and enlightening as a yoga class. And the truth is, if you can make a great meatball, nothing else really matters.

Pollo alla Contadini

Peasant chicken, farmer's wife's chicken, whatever its name, poultry simmered in a seasoned tomato sauce is one of my winter staples. I make it with a cut-up chicken for family, but it's not the prettiest way to present for company. Cornish hens are something else altogether. Ask your butcher to tie the hens for you; otherwise, tuck the wings underneath the legs and tie them together with kitchen string. I always prepare this in a big lidded copper pan and serve directly from it, family-style. (See photo page 130.)

SERVES 4 TO 6

YOU'LL NEED:
kitchen string

2 ounces dried porcini

4 small Cornish hens
(1¼–1½ pounds each)

Flour, for dredging

⅓ cup olive oil

¼ cup unsalted butter

1 cup dry white wine

2 cups large pearl onions, peeled

18 tiny carrots, greens trimmed

6 celery stalks with leaves, halved lengthwise and cut into 1" pieces

1 (35-ounce) can crushed San Marzano tomatoes

12 sage leaves, chopped

8 basil leaves, torn

2 tablespoons fresh rosemary

Kosher salt and freshly ground black pepper

COVER THE PORCINI with hot water and soak 20 to 30 minutes, until well softened. Lift the porcini out with a slotted spoon, squeezing the liquid into the bowl. Strain the soaking liquid through a sieve lined with a damp paper towel and reserve.

WASH THE HENS and pat dry. Put the flour on a large plate and roll the hens around in it until they are lightly coated. Shake off the excess flour.

HEAT THE OIL and butter in a wide, high-sided lidded pan over medium-high heat. Brown the hens all over, making sure the skin is deep golden, about 10 minutes total. Remove the hens to a platter. Pour the wine into the pan and cook until all but a few tablespoons evaporate. Add the onions and cook about 5 minutes, until soft and golden. Add the porcini, carrots, and celery and cook 5 minutes more. Return the hens to the pan, breast-side up, and add the tomatoes, sage, basil, and rosemary. Season generously with salt and pepper and stir gently to incorporate. Bring to a gentle boil, then reduce the heat and simmer, partially covered, about 1 hour, stirring occasionally, until the vegetables are soft and the hens' juices run clear. Add the reserved porcini soaking liquid as needed to keep the hens moist. Serve the hen and vegetables with some of the sauce ladled on top.

Filet Mignon with Gorgonzola Sauce

At the risk of sounding trite, I have yet to meet a man who doesn't love a good steak. While filet is considered the king of beef cuts, it's easy to ruin because it's not marbled with fat the way other cuts are. This is a somewhat counterintuitive method used by steakhouse chefs and one you should memorize if you want to make your way to Mr. X's heart. It yields the juiciest steak you can imagine. If you have 2 large skillets, you can make it for 4. Whatever you do, don't cover the pan or the steak will steam rather than sear.

SERVES 2

2 (12-ounce) filet mignon steaks, about 2" thick

Extra-virgin olive oil

Kosher salt and freshly ground black pepper

1¼ cups heavy cream

2 ounces Gorgonzola, crumbled

2 teaspoons snipped chives

PAT THE STEAKS DRY WITH paper towels and brush both sides generously with olive oil. Set aside at room temperature for 1 to 1½ hours.

PLACE A LARGE, HEAVY OVENPROOF SAUTÉ PAN over high heat. (If your skillet's handle is not ovenproof, wrap it in foil before placing it in the oven.) Season one side of each steak generously with salt and pepper. When the pan is really hot, place the steaks in the pan with tongs, seasoned side down. Do not move them or press down on them. (This makes it important to get the placement in the pan right the first time. Once they're in, you're not moving them until they are ready to turn.) Cook for 2½ minutes, then season the top of the steaks with salt and pepper and turn them over. Cook for another 2½ minutes. Transfer the steaks to a wire rack set over a plate and let stand at room temperature for 30 minutes. Don't wash the pan.

PREHEAT THE OVEN to 425°F.

TO MAKE THE SAUCE, bring the cream to a simmer in a small saucepan and cook for 4 minutes, until thickened. Remove from the heat and stir in the Gorgonzola, chives, and a little pepper.

RETURN THE STEAKS to the pan in which they were seared, and finish cooking in the oven, 12 minutes for medium-rare or 15 minutes for medium. Transfer to the rack again and let rest for 5 to 8 minutes. Serve on warm plates topped with a spoonful of the sauce. Pass the remaining sauce on the side.

Scampi Ribelli (Rebellious Shrimp)

I've never been able to track down the genesis of the notion that combining shellfish and cheese is a culinary sin, but I can tell you from experience that in Puglia the two show up in dishes all the time—thus the name of this dish. My father created it for his first Long Island restaurant, La Tavernetta, where it stayed on the menu for 37 years and with good reason: It's delicious. He continues to serve it to this day at his Manhattan restaurant, Fiorini.

SERVES 4 TO 6

¼ cup extra-virgin olive oil plus more for drizzling

1 cup fresh bread crumbs made from stale Italian bread

¼ cup freshly grated pecorino cheese

⅓ cup fresh thyme leaves, stripped from the stems and coarsely chopped

2 large garlic cloves, minced

Freshly ground black pepper

1½ pounds large shrimp, peeled and deveined

2 large lemons, each cut into 6 wedges

PREHEAT THE OVEN to 450°F. Slick a large baking sheet with oil.

COMBINE THE BREAD CRUMBS, pecorino, thyme, garlic, and pepper to taste in a bowl. Stir in the ¼ cup of olive oil to moisten the bread crumbs.

ARRANGE THE SHRIMP on the baking sheet in a single layer. Spoon a little of the bread crumb mixture onto each shrimp. Bake until the crumbs are golden brown and the shrimp are cooked through, about 10 minutes.

TRANSFER THE SHRIMP to a serving platter using a spatula. Drizzle a little olive oil over them and garnish with the lemon wedges.

Tilapia Oreganata

Not only is this the most forgiving fish dish I know, it's among the easiest to pull together, *and* it's easy on the wallet. Oreganata is a preparation seen all over Italy, but every home cook seems to have a different recipe for the herb mixture. Believe me when I tell you that if you were to ask for the recipe, any self-respecting Italian cook would "accidentally" leave out a key ingredient. My mix includes pecorino cheese and panko crumbs, two ingredients you won't find in any version in Italy. Serve with "Fried" Cauliflower (page 179).

SERVES 4

4 (6-ounce) tilapia fillets

Extra-virgin olive oil

¾ cup fine, dried bread crumbs such as panko flakes

1 garlic clove, minced

1 teaspoon dried oregano

1 teaspoon chopped fresh mint

1 teaspoon chopped fresh parsley

2 tablespoons grated pecorino cheese

Kosher salt and freshly ground black pepper

Fresh herb leaves, such as mint and parsley, for garnish

Lemon wedges

PREHEAT THE OVEN to 350°F.

SLICK EACH FILLET with a thin coat of olive oil and set on a baking sheet. Combine the panko, garlic, oregano, mint, parsley, pecorino, and salt and pepper in a small bowl. Dredge the fish in the mixture, covering each from end to end. Bake for 10 minutes and remove from the oven.

PREHEAT THE BROILER with the oven rack 5" from the heat source. Drizzle 3 tablespoons of the olive oil over the fillets and broil until the crumbs are browned, 30 seconds to 1 minute. Arrange 2 fillets on each plate and garnish with the mint and parsley and lemon wedges.

Mama's Meatballs

Heels off for this one, ladies. I make these meatballs on Sundays, and it's an all-day commitment. Should you make them, I promise it will pay off. You won't be standing at the stove for hours; there's more simmering than hands-on cooking going on. The meatballs and ragù take me back to the Sundays of my childhood. I would wake up not to the smell of bacon and eggs but to garlic and onions, which meant that the whole family, including my father who worked 6 days a week, was going to be home all day.

Fast-forward 3 decades and my mother's meatballs continue to be a favorite at Mia Dona, where they've won raves from the *New York Times*, *Time Out New York*, and *New York Magazine*. You can't go wrong with them, especially if you're hosting a crowd.

SERVES 8 TO 10

Ragù

¼ cup extra-virgin olive oil

2 celery stalks, with leaves, chopped

1 medium onion, chopped

Kosher salt and freshly ground black pepper

1½ pounds (about 8) meaty, bone-in pork spareribs, rinsed

1½ pounds (6–8) sweet Italian sausage with fennel seeds, pierced all over with a fork

1 garlic clove, chopped

1 cup red wine

3 (35-ounce) cans tomato puree

Handful of fresh basil leaves

Meatballs and Spaghetti

1 small loaf stale Italian bread (about 8 thick slices), torn into 2½" chunks (see the Chef Tip, page 142)

2 pounds 80% lean ground beef chuck, broken up

5 garlic cloves, coarsely chopped

½ cup finely chopped flat-leaf parsley

1 large egg, lightly beaten

1½ cups grated Parmigiano-Reggiano or Grana Padano

Kosher salt and freshly ground black pepper

Canola oil for frying

2 pounds spaghetti

TO MAKE THE SAUCE: Warm the olive oil in a large, heavy-bottomed pot over medium heat. Add the celery and onion, generously season with salt and pepper, and sauté, partially covered, about 5 minutes, until golden and soft. Add the ribs and sausage in a single layer, raise the heat to medium-high and sauté, again partially covered, turning occasionally until the meat is nicely browned all over. Add the garlic and cook until fragrant, about 1 minute. Add the wine and cook until it evaporates, about 5 minutes. Add the tomato puree and the basil and season generously with salt and pepper. Partially cover, bring to a boil, then reduce the heat and let the sauce simmer quietly for 1½ to 2 hours, adjusting the heat as necessary to prevent it from boiling.

TO MAKE THE MEATBALLS AND SPAGHETTI: Put the bread in a bowl and add enough warm water to cover the bread. Let stand for 5 minutes, turning to moisten evenly. Squeeze gently to remove as much water as possible from the bread chunks (they will fall apart, which is okay) and place in a large bowl.

ADD THE BEEF, garlic, parsley, egg, and ¾ cup of the Parmigiano to the bread and combine. Season generously with salt and pepper. Knead the mixture with your hands, rinsing your hands under warm water occasionally to keep the meat from sticking to them, until it is uniformly combined and smooth. This will take at least 5 minutes.

PINCH A TABLESPOON of the meat from the mound and shape it into a ball between the palms of your hands. Place on a baking sheet or tray and repeat with the remaining meat mixture. You should have about 30 meatballs.

FILL A 10" SKILLET halfway with canola oil and heat over high heat. You will see strands forming along the bottom of the pan when it is hot enough. Working in batches, gently slide 8 to 10 meatballs into the skillet without overcrowding the pan. The meatballs should be only three-quarters submerged in the oil. Reduce the heat to medium and fry, turning once, until they are firm and golden, 12 to 14 minutes total. Use a slotted spoon to transfer the meatballs to a bowl (placing them on paper towels drains them of their delicious juices). Raise the heat to high in between batches to ensure the oil is hot when you slide the meatballs into it. Twenty minutes before serving, add the meatballs to the simmering tomato sauce; you don't want them to soak up too much of the liquid and become soggy.

BRING A LARGE POT of generously salted water to a boil. Add the pasta and cook according to package directions until al dente. Drain in a colander and return to the pot.

REMOVE THE MEATBALLS and pork ribs from the ragù using a slotted spoon and transfer to a rimmed serving platter. Add about 1 cup of the ragù and the remaining ¾ cup Parmigiano to the pasta in the pot and toss until evenly distributed. Place the platter of meatballs and ribs and a large bowl of sauce on the table and serve with individual plates of pasta, each topped with a ladleful of sauce.

chef tip

The best bread for this is the super market Italian bread that comes in a white paper bag. Choose a regular (not semolina), unseeded loaf. If the bread is very fresh, remove the crust and dry for 30 minutes in a 200°F oven.

Cherry Tomato, Mint, Asparagus, and Gruyère Frittata

In Italy, frittatas are typically eaten at the lighter evening meal (lunch is the main meal of the day), but I find they are perfectly appropriate for brunch, picnics, lunch, or dinner American-style—even cut into small bites for hors d'oeuvres. Humble as it may seem, this mixture of eggs, vegetables, and cheese puffs up soufflé-style thanks to the addition of beaten egg whites, to bring a little drama to the table. Serve this with Herb-Tied Salad (page 61) and Pan-Fried New Potatoes with Chorizo (page 186).

SERVES 4 TO 6

YOU'LL NEED:
electric mixer

8 extra-large eggs

½ cup light cream

½ cup grated Parmigiano-Reggiano

½ cup grated Gruyère

½ cup basil leaves, torn into bite-sized pieces plus a few sprigs for garnish

½ cup mint leaves, torn into bite-sized pieces

Kosher salt and freshly ground black pepper

2 tablespoons extra-virgin olive oil

½ pound slender asparagus, ends trimmed, chopped into ½" pieces

1 pint cherry tomatoes, halved lengthwise

PREHEAT THE OVEN to 425°F with a rack in the center.

SEPARATE 4 of the eggs, placing the yolks in a medium bowl and the whites in a large one. Add the remaining 4 eggs to the yolks and whisk in the cream, Parmigiano, Gruyère, basil, and mint. Beat the egg whites with a clean whisk or electric mixer until they form stiff peaks. Fold the egg whites into the egg mixture until there are no streaks. Season with salt and pepper and set aside.

HEAT THE OLIVE OIL in a large, ovenproof skillet over medium-high heat. Add the asparagus and cook about 3 minutes, until they are slightly softened and bright green. Add the tomatoes and cook about 2 minutes more, until they are softened. Pour the egg mixture into the pan and cook, lifting the edges with a spatula to allow the uncooked egg to flow to the bottom of the pan. Cook until the edges of the frittata are firm and the center is still a bit runny, 7 to 10 minutes, then transfer the pan to the oven and bake about 8 minutes, until set, puffed, and golden. Cool slightly, then cut into wedges and garnish each with a few sprigs of basil.

Robiola Pizza

My palate lost its virginity at Da Ciro, a midtown Manhattan pizzeria, many years ago. My cousin pushed me to branch out from my standard pizza margherita order to something a bit more adventuresome. It sounds corny, but to this day, I dream about the robiola and truffle oil pizza I first tasted there.

This is a fantastic pizza, but it relies almost entirely on the robiola cheese (okay, the white truffle oil does its thing, too) for its impact. If you can't find robiola, please don't substitute another cheese—it just won't be as good! And be *sure* to use truffle oil—the combination of robiola and truffle oil is magical. Instead of taking the time to make my own dough, I take the easy route by buying it from my neighborhood pizzaria. Ask your neighborhood pizza place if it will sell you a pound of pizza dough (you can also buy French or Italian bread dough from a bakery—the doughs are basically the same thing). The dough will last for 24 hours in your refrigerator. Remove from the refrigerator and let stand for 1 to 2 hours to bring it to cool room temperature, when it will begin to puff up.

Depending on the size of the wedges, the pizza can be served with a simple green salad for a casual kind of night or cut into two-bite pieces for hors d'oeuvres.

SERVES 4 TO 6

YOU'LL NEED: parchment paper, rolling pin

1 pound pizza dough, at cool room temperature

10 ounces robiola cheese, rind removed, at room temperature

Sea salt and freshly ground black pepper

⅔ cup baby arugula, coarsely chopped

2–3 teaspoons white truffle oil

ABOUT 30 MINUTES before baking the pizza, preheat the oven to 500°F and place a large, rimless (or upside down) baking sheet in the lower third of the oven.

PLACE A LARGE SHEET of parchment paper on a work surface and dust the parchment lightly with flour. Roll the dough out using a rolling pin (if the dough resists rolling, cover it with a towel and let it relax for 5 minutes). Pierce the dough firmly all over with the tines of a fork. Slide the whole thing, including the parchment, onto a rimless baking sheet, then slide it onto the hot baking sheet in the oven. When the dough is slightly puffed but not golden, about 7 to 8 minutes, push down any bubbles with the back of a spoon and bake for 2 minutes more.

GRAB THE EDGE of the parchment and transfer the pizza from the oven to a cutting board, again using a rimless baking sheet or the back of a rimmed pan to facilitate moving it. Place one hand on top of the pizza, using a folded kitchen towel to protect your hand from the heat, and use a serrated knife to split the dough into 2 thin horizontal layers. Keep the knife parallel to the work surface, and don't worry if you go through the top layer in a couple of places. Set aside the top layer and spread the bottom with the softened cheese. Season with salt and pepper and top with the arugula. Replace the top layer and press down gently. Slide the pizza back into the oven for 2 minutes more, or until the top is slightly golden.

REMOVE FROM THE OVEN and drizzle with the truffle oil. Cut in half crosswise, then cut each half into wedges and serve warm.

Yellowtail alla Plancha

For more than a decade, Nobu Matsuhisa's namesake restaurant has been one of the hottest meals in town, not least because he makes the world's best miso-glazed cod. This dish is inspired by his, but draws on my Mediterranean heritage. I've used both fig balsamic vinegar and vincotto (cooked wine) for the sweet glaze, and a fish fit for entertaining—satiny, luxurious yellowtail.

SERVES 4

YOU'LL NEED: cast-iron stovetop grill pan

4 dried figs, stems removed

¼ cup white or red wine or vermouth

12 ramps or young scallions, root ends trimmed

2 tablespoons extra-virgin olive oil

1¼ pounds yellowtail or red snapper fillets

Kosher salt and freshly ground black pepper

4 tablespoons fig balsamic vinegar or vincotto (see Chef Tip)

CUT THE FIGS into ¼" dice and place in a small bowl with the wine. Set aside to soak.

CUT AWAY ANY DRIED OR BROKEN ENDS of scallion leaves; cut off about 2" of the white parts, reserving both parts. Warm the oil in a skillet over low heat and add the bulbs. Cover and sauté, shaking the pan, until golden and slightly tender, about 8 minutes. Add the greens, reduce the heat to low, and cook, covered, shaking the pan occasionally, until tender, about 10 minutes.

MEANWHILE, HEAT A CAST-IRON STOVETOP GRILL PAN over medium-high heat. Season both sides of the fillets with salt and pepper. Grill skin side down for 4 to 5 minutes without moving; turn over and grill for 4 to 5 minutes more, until opaque in the center.

DRAIN THE FIGS. Serve the fish topped with some of the diced figs, the scallions, and a generous drizzle of fig balsamic vinegar or vincotto.

chef tip: make your own

If you can't find fig balsamic or vincotto (see page 74 for an online source), place 1 cup of balsamic vinegar in a small saucepan and cook over medium heat until it's reduced by about half and has the consistency of syrup.

Lamb Chops with Lemon-Mint Gremolata

If you can turn on the broiler, you can turn out these tender little chops with less effort than it takes to order in. They're relatively pricey, but if time is your most precious commodity, as it is mine, they're beyond worth it. Before you have your heart set on serving lamb, make sure your guests eat it; not everyone loves it. Look for chops that are firm and pink with good marbling and moist, reddish bones. Serve with Roasted Asparagus with Parmigiano-Reggiano (page 184) and Warm Potatoes with Arugula and Fresh Herbs (page 190).

SERVES 4 TO 6

YOU'LL NEED:
Microplane zester

2–3 rib lamb chops per guest

Extra-virgin olive oil

Kosher salt and freshly ground black pepper

Grated zest of 2 lemons

1 large shallot, finely chopped

2 garlic cloves, finely chopped

1 tablespoon finely chopped fresh mint

Lemon extra-virgin olive oil, for drizzling (optional)

BRUSH THE LAMB CHOPS all over with olive oil and season both sides generously with salt and pepper. Set aside at room temperature for at least 20 minutes or up to 1 hour.

COMBINE THE LEMON ZEST, shallot, garlic, and mint in a small bowl. Set the gremolata aside.

PREHEAT THE BROILER with the oven rack 5" to 6" from the heat source. Place the chops on a rimmed baking sheet or broiler pan outfitted with a rack. When the broiler is very hot, broil the chops for 4 minutes on each side. Turn off the broiler but leave the chops in the oven with the door closed. Let the chops rest for 10 minutes for medium-rare or 15 minutes for medium. Arrange 2 or 3 of the chops on each plate, drizzle with lemon olive oil, and garnish with the gremolata.

donatella clicks

If you can't find good lamb chops locally, visit www.lavalake-lamb.com. The Idaho-based purveyor sells fresh, certified organic, grass-fed lamb loin chops ready to broil as soon as they show up at your door.

Seared Ahi with Watercress and Yogurt Sauce

There's so little to this that it's essential to buy only fine-quality tuna from a reputable purveyor. If the fish is top-notch, the only detail remaining is to be sure you don't overcook it. The flesh should remain jewel-toned on the inside, with just a slender rim of gray (cooked tuna) surrounding it. You can serve the sauce on the side, or do as chefs do and dispense it from a squeeze bottle to make elegant designs on the plate. Serve this with Quinoa, Tabbouleh-Style (page 185).

SERVES 4 TO 6

YOU'LL NEED:
cast-iron stovetop grill pan

2 cups loosely packed watercress, thick stems discarded

1 cup full-fat plain Greek yogurt

¼ cup mayonnaise

2 garlic cloves, smashed and very finely chopped

3 teaspoons fresh lemon juice

¼ teaspoon ground cumin

Kosher salt and ground white pepper

1 tablespoon olive oil

4–6 ahi tuna steaks, about 5 ounces each and 1¼" thick, halved lengthwise

Freshly ground black pepper

PULL THE LEAVES off the stems of 1 cup of the watercress and discard the stems. Combine the leaves with the yogurt, mayonnaise, garlic, 2 teaspoons of the lemon juice, the cumin, ½ teaspoon salt, and ½ teaspoon white pepper. Whisk until blended. Cover and refrigerate for up to 2 hours.

COMBINE THE REMAINING 1 teaspoon lemon juice and the olive oil in a medium bowl and set aside. Meanwhile, preheat a cast-iron stovetop grill pan over medium-high heat. Season both sides of the tuna steaks lightly with salt and black pepper. Grill for about 4 minutes on each side, rotating half a turn halfway through the cooking time on each side to create cross-hatch grill marks. Just before serving, toss the remaining watercress in the vinaigrette. Place a tuna steak on each plate, top with some dressed watercress, and serve with a large spoonful of the yogurt sauce on the side.

Straccetti (Little Rags)

I was never a big steak eater until my friend Giancarlo Quadiale, chef of Bianca in New York City, made this for me, and I was knocked out. Unlike grilled steak, this isn't heavy at all. For speed and simplicity, this Roman specialty is hard to beat, especially if you ask your butcher to slice the rib eye paper-thin for you. You may want to order the extra-thick steak from him or her in advance—and consider using dry-aged beef for even more intense flavor. It's a great way to share an amazing cut of meat without blowing your budget.

SERVES 4 TO 6

1 (2"-thick) boneless rib-eye steak, 1¾–2 pounds, trimmed of exterior fat and cut crosswise into ¼" x 2" strips

2 tablespoons extra-virgin olive oil

Kosher salt and freshly ground black pepper

2 tablespoons chopped flat-leaf parsley

6 large garlic cloves, smashed with the side of a heavy knife

4 sprigs fresh rosemary, needles removed from 2 and chopped

Lemon extra-virgin olive oil or truffle oil, for drizzling

Half a lemon, for serving

DIVIDE THE BEEF SLICES between 2 large pieces of aluminum foil, arranging them in a single layer, and refrigerate them until ready to cook.

WARM THE OLIVE OIL in a very large skillet or sauté pan over medium heat. Meanwhile, remove the meat from the refrigerator and season with the salt, pepper, and parsley. Add the garlic and chopped rosemary to the hot oil and cook until soft and fragrant, about 30 seconds. Put 1 batch of the meat into the pan by flipping the foil directly over the pan so that the meat falls into the pan. Sauté, tossing with tongs, for less then 30 seconds. Transfer to a serving platter, let the oil reheat for a few seconds, then sauté the second batch of "rags" in the same way. Transfer to the platter and top with the garlic and rosemary from the pan. Drizzle with a little lemon olive oil and a squeeze of lemon. Garnish with the rosemary sprigs and serve.

donatella clicks

I half-jokingly refer to Lobel's (www.lobels.com) on Manhattan's Upper East Side as the meat museum. There's no more beautiful butcher shop around. They gladly ship anywhere in the country.

Veal Scallops with Eggplant and Melting Mozzarella

A veal scallop is just as easy to cook as a chicken breast, yet it delivers a bit more culinary cachet. The veal layered with eggplant and oozing mozzarella is both down-to-earth and sophisticated. Trim the veal of excess fat around the edge to prevent it from curling when you sauté it. Serve this with Tomato Gratin (page 189). If you have 2 very large skillets, you can easily double the recipe to serve 4. Wrap the handles in foil if your skillets are not oven-safe.

SERVES 4 TO 6

1 Japanese or small eggplant, sliced lengthwise about ⅜" thick

Kosher salt and freshly ground black pepper

3 tablespoons olive oil

1 cup all-purpose flour

2 veal scallops (3–4 ounces each)

1 tablespoon white wine

5 ounces fresh mozzarella (preferably buffalo mozzarella), sliced

¼ cup bottled tomato or marinara-style sauce, warmed

6 fresh basil leaves

SEASON THE EGGPLANT SLICES with salt and pepper. Heat 2 tablespoons of the olive oil in a large, ovenproof skillet over medium-high heat. Sauté the eggplant about 2 minutes per side, until golden brown. Remove to a plate and set aside.

PREHEAT THE BROILER with the oven rack 6" from the heat source.

DUMP THE FLOUR on a dinner plate. Season the veal generously with salt and pepper, then dredge in the flour. Add the remaining tablespoon of olive oil to the pan and sauté the veal until golden brown on both sides, about 3 minutes total, turning once. Drizzle the wine around the rim of the pan. Place a slice of eggplant on top of each veal scallop, then top with a slice of mozzarella. Place the skillet under the broiler until the cheese melts. Place 1 veal scallop on each dinner plate, spoon a little tomato sauce over each, and garnish with the basil.

donatella clicks

After decades of customers boycotting inhumanely raised veal, farmers have taken note: Grass-fed veal raised humanely is increasingly available. If you live near a green market, try the meat purveyor there. Order it online at Bobolink Dairy Farm (www.cowsoutside.com).

Grilled Whole Branzino with Sizzling Hazelnut Butter

I've auditioned dozens of chefs for my restaurants, inviting them into the kitchen to let them show me how creative they can be. My method is never to restrict what they're going to do so I let them prepare whatever they think will dazzle me. A few years back, one particular chef's tasting wasn't going well at all—until he presented me with a whole grilled fish over which he poured hazelnuts sizzling in butter. He ultimately didn't get the job, but I have him to thank for the inspiration for this recipe. The key to no-tears, no-stick grilling of fish is a very hot grill and a very cold fish—that and resisting the urge to move the fish around once it hits the grill. Serve with Warm Potatoes with Arugula and Fresh Herbs (page 190).

SERVES 4 TO 6

YOU'LL NEED:
cast-iron
stovetop grill
pan

---

2 tablespoons extra-virgin olive oil plus more for brushing on the grill

2 tablespoons unsalted butter

½ cup coarsely chopped hazelnuts

6 garlic cloves, thinly sliced

¼ cup chopped fresh thyme leaves

¼ cup chopped flat-leaf parsley

4–6 whole branzino or red snapper (½ pound each), gutted and scaled by your fishmonger, chilled

½ lemon, thinly sliced

Kosher salt and freshly ground black pepper

Small handful chopped fresh herbs, such as dill, parsley, basil, and/or chives, for garnish

---

HEAT A CAST-IRON STOVETOP GRILL PAN over very high heat and brush lightly with olive oil.

COMBINE THE OLIVE OIL, butter, and hazelnuts in a small saucepan and cook over medium heat until the butter is melted. Set aside. Combine the garlic, thyme, and parsley in a bowl. Just before you are ready to grill, stuff the cavity of the very cold fish with the garlic mixture and the lemon slices; season both sides lightly with salt and pepper. Grill until nicely charred, about 3 to 5 minutes on each side, depending on the thickness. Insert a metal skewer near the backbone for a few moments to test for doneness. Hold the tip of the skewer against your lower lip: If the skewer is warm, the fish is done. Transfer to a large platter.

RETURN THE BUTTER MIXTURE to medium heat and cook until it sizzles. Pour over the fish at the table, then garnish with the chopped herbs.

Salmon in Cartoccio with Caponata

Salmon cooked in parchment (*al cartoccio*) is healthy, delicious, foolproof, and dramatic. Use the technique with almost any combination of fish, aromatic herbs, and a little liquid such as wine or sweet vermouth, and the results will always be the same: super-moist, flavorful, and intact. Aluminum foil does the same job, but save it for when you're cooking in sweatpants and slippers.

Caponata is a sweet-and-sour ratatouille-like condiment of eggplant, zucchini, and spices. Any gourmet food store carries it. Contorni makes the best jarred variety I've come across. I always serve the fish in the packets, but if you decide to plate the fish in the kitchen and remove the parchment so it won't clutter up the table, be sure to slide the fish and all the sauce onto the plate (instead of using a spatula). You don't want to leave any juice behind.

SERVES 4

YOU'LL NEED:
parchment
paper

12 ounces Italian-style caponata, from a jar or the refrigerated section, well drained

¼ teaspoon dried Greek or wild oregano

1½ tablespoons finely chopped fresh herbs, such as dill, flat-leaf parsley, or basil

1½ teaspoons white wine vinegar

4 wild salmon fillets (about 6 ounces each)

Kosher salt and freshly ground black pepper

2 teaspoons white wine or vermouth

PREHEAT THE OVEN to 400°F.

IF THE CHUNKS of caponata are very large, cut them into ½" cubes. Combine with the oregano, fresh herbs, and vinegar. Season each fillet on both sides with a little salt and plenty of pepper. Cut 4 sheets of parchment paper about 12" long. Fold in half, then open up and place a salmon fillet on one side of the fold. Spoon the caponata evenly over the top of each fillet, then drizzle with ½ teaspoon white wine. Fold the parchment over the fish and, beginning at one of the corners, crimp, roll, and fold the edges of the parchment to make a well-sealed package. Place on a baking sheet and roast for 12 minutes. Let rest for 5 minutes, then transfer the packages directly onto plates. Slash the top open just a little to expose the salmon inside. Provide a bowl for guests to dispose of the parchment.

Almond-Crusted Chicken Paillards

I ate chicken cutlets as a child the way kids today eat chicken nuggets. Not a week went by when my mother didn't make them. I'd eat one for dinner and put another between 2 pieces of Wonder bread slathered with mayonnaise for lunch the next day. It wasn't until many years later, while vacationing in Capri, that I encountered a version that was chic enough to serve at a dinner party. This way boneless, skinless chicken breasts cook through evenly without drying out. Don't put the tomato salad on top of the cutlet until just before serving to avoid a soggy crust.

SERVES 4 TO 6

YOU'LL NEED:
meat mallet or rolling pin, mini food processor, 2 (12") skillets

4 (6-ounce) boneless, skinless chicken breast halves

Kosher salt and freshly ground black pepper

⅔ cup sliced unblanched almonds

⅔ cup panko bread crumbs

1 teaspoon minced fresh tarragon or ½ teaspoon dried

2 large eggs

20 cherry tomatoes, red or yellow, halved

2 scallions, trimmed and thinly sliced

2 tablespoons fresh lemon juice

4 tablespoons extra-virgin olive oil

1 tablespoon unsalted butter, melted

Lemon wedges for serving

PAT THE CHICKEN BREASTS dry with paper towels. Place each breast between 2 sheets of plastic wrap, opening out the fillets or "tenders." Pound gently with a mallet or rolling pin to an even thickness, working out from the center. Do not make them thinner than about ⅜". Season both sides generously with salt and pepper.

PULSE THE ALMONDS a few times in a mini or standard food processor until coarsely chopped; do not pulverize. Combine the almonds on a plate with the panko and half of the tarragon. Lightly whisk the eggs in a shallow bowl with a pinch of salt. Dip each piece of chicken into the eggs, letting the excess drip away, then press both sides of the chicken into the panko coating. Place on a baking sheet and refrigerate for at least 20 minutes to set the crust. Meanwhile, put the tomatoes and scallions in a bowl and add the lemon juice, 2 tablespoons of the olive oil, and the remaining tarragon. Toss to coat and set aside.

HEAT A 12" SKILLET over medium heat and add the butter and the remaining 2 tablespoons of olive oil. When the butter has foamed, place the chicken in the pan and increase the heat to medium-high. Cook, turning once, until the crust sets and turns golden brown, 3 to 3½ minutes on each side. Cut the pillards in halves or thirds, arrange on a platter, and serve immediately with the tomato salad spooned on top and garnished with lemon wedges.

Family-Style Polenta with Bolognese

I have a great group of Italian men friends whom I refer to as the gigolos—they're in their 40s and still chasing models half their age. It's no wonder the pretty young things are won over, though, because their ringleader, Raffaelo, throws *the best* parties in their loft in Manhattan's Meatpacking District. They really know how to cook and entertain without looking like it takes any effort. This homey, sexy dish is a great example of their cooking. All over Northern Italy, polenta is served family-style, spread on a board accompanied by Bolognese and cheese or other toppings.

I find I gravitate to this dish when I want to gather close friends I haven't seen since Memorial Day, when everyone seems to take flight for the summer. Serve it with a pitcher of sangria or fruity Italian red wine and a simple green salad.

SERVES 4 TO 6

YOU'LL NEED: parchment paper

Bolognese Sauce

3 tablespoons olive oil

1 small white onion, finely chopped

1 small carrot, finely chopped

1 celery rib, finely chopped

1 garlic clove, minced

2 bay leaves

6 ounces ground veal

6 ounces lean ground pork

½ cup full-bodied red wine

1 (28-ounce) can diced plum tomatoes, preferably Italian, with their juice

½ cup heavy cream

Kosher salt and freshly ground black pepper

¼ teaspoon ground nutmeg

¼ cup grated Parmigiano-Reggiano

4 large basil leaves, cut into chiffonade (see page 30)

Polenta

4½ cups low-sodium chicken broth

1½ cups milk

2 teaspoons kosher salt

1 (13-ounce) package instant polenta

6 ounces kasseri or soft pecorino cheese, shaved with a vegetable peeler

Freshly ground black pepper

Fresh oregano or basil leaves for garnish

TO MAKE THE BOLOGNESE: Heat the oil in a large, heavy-bottomed pot over medium-low heat. Add the onion, carrot, and celery, and cook about 5 minutes, until the onions are translucent. Add the garlic and bay leaves, and cook for 1 minute more. Add the veal and pork and cook, stirring to break up any chunks, until the meat is no longer pink, about 7 minutes. Add the wine, raise the heat to high, and cook until the liquid is reduced slightly, about 5 minutes. Add the tomatoes and their juice and the cream and reduce the heat to low. Cook, uncovered, for about 1 hour, stirring every 10 minutes or so. Season with ¾ teaspoon salt, plenty of pepper, and the nutmeg. The sauce should be very thick and chunky. If it isn't, increase the heat and cook for 10 minutes more. Season to taste with salt and pepper. Stir in the Parmigiano and the basil and remove the bay leaves.

TO MAKE THE POLENTA: Combine the chicken broth, milk, and salt in a large, heavy saucepan and place over medium-high heat. Bring the liquid to a simmer, then gradually sprinkle the polenta over it in a very slow, thin stream, whisking constantly in the same direction until all the grains are incorporated and no lumps remain. Reduce the heat to low and cook, stirring with a wooden spoon, until the polenta is so thick that the spoon stands on its own, 5 to 6 minutes.

TO SERVE, SCOOP the warm polenta onto a large wooden parchment paper–lined serving tray or cutting board and smooth into a thick oval. Arrange the kasseri cheese on one end of the oval and the warm Bolognese sauce on the other. Grind pepper over all, garnish with oregano or basil, and serve immediately, with a large serving spoon.

chef tip: real cheese

Italians never eat skim, low-fat, or fake, processed cheeses. These items have no place in a proper Mediterranean diet. What *does* belong is eating a little of the real stuff and enjoying it. Let me tell you, I know all about wanting to lose 10 pounds, but the phony food route is not the way there. Fake food won't satisfy you, and you'll end up eating more. Better to indulge a little and actually feel like you've treated yourself.

Halibut in Phyllo with Porcini, Spinach, and Feta

As far as I'm concerned, good things, especially food, come in packages—any size is fine. I love peeling back the wrapping with my fork to find a surprise inside. This fish dish is inspired by the classic Greek mezze, spanakopita—phyllo triangles filled with spinach and feta. The phyllo keeps the buttery fish insanely moist. Be sure to give frozen phyllo at least 2 and up to 3 hours to thaw at room temperature. Don't try to hurry the process or the delicate sheets of pastry may crack or stick to one another. Extra phyllo may be refrozen.

SERVES 4

5 tablespoons extra-virgin olive oil

5 ounces porcini mushrooms, cleaned and thickly sliced

3 garlic cloves, very finely chopped

2 cups (2–3 ounces) washed and dried baby spinach leaves

2 scallions, thinly sliced

2 ounces (about ⅓ cup) Greek feta, crumbled

Kosher salt and freshly ground black pepper

¼ cup (½ stick) unsalted butter

16 sheets phyllo dough, from a 1-pound box, thawed

4 (4-ounce) halibut fillets

HEAT 2 TABLESPOONS of the olive oil in a large skillet over medium-high heat. Add the mushrooms and sauté about 3 minutes, until tender. Add the garlic and cook for 30 seconds, then stir in the spinach and scallions and cook until the spinach has wilted. Remove from the heat and stir in the feta. Season lightly with salt and plenty of pepper. Warm the remaining 3 tablespoons olive oil with the butter in a small saucepan. Remove from the heat.

PREHEAT THE OVEN to 375°F.

UNROLL THE PHYLLO dough and cover with a barely damp towel. On a dry surface, layer 4 sheets of phyllo, fanning each slightly to the right and painting each sheet lightly with the oil-butter mixture before placing the next sheet on top. Place a square of halibut fillet in the center, season lightly with salt and pepper and top with one-quarter of the porcini mixture (don't worry if some spills over the side). Bring all 4 sides of the pastry up over the fish and pinch together to form a fanned purse. Transfer to a nonstick baking sheet and repeat to make 3 more packages. Paint the outsides of the packages with a little more oil-butter and bake for 22 minutes. Transfer to plates and serve.

Roasted Rack of Pork with Cabbage and Bacon

When the family makes plans to gather at your house, put this roast on the menu. It may conjure images of June Cleaver circa 1950 but there's a reason she smiled as she set the big platter down on the table: A properly cooked roast is a beautiful, impressive thing. And when the rest of the meal is roasted right in the same pan, even more so. Take care not to overcook the pork; it should be slightly pink in the center.

SERVES 6 TO 8

YOU'LL NEED: roasting pan with rack

1 (5½-pound) pork loin on the bone, rack removed and tied back on (have the butcher do this)

Kosher salt and freshly ground black pepper

½ cup extra-virgin olive oil

3 apples, peeled, cored, and cut into 6 wedges

14 scallions, trimmed

½ pound bacon, diced

6 garlic cloves, smashed

6 sage leaves, chopped

2 tablespoons chopped rosemary needles

3 tablespoons butter

1 head Savoy cabbage, trimmed of outer leaves and torn into large pieces

4 sprigs thyme

1 cup apple cider

Juice of 1 lemon

PREHEAT THE OVEN to 450°F and position a rack in the center.

SEASON THE PORK generously all over with salt and pepper. Heat ¼ cup of the olive oil in a large, heavy-bottomed pot over medium-high heat. Sear the roast on all sides, beginning with the fatty side, until lightly browned all over. Set the roast, bone side down, on a rack in a roasting pan and roast for 15 minutes. Reduce the temperature to 350°F and roast for 30 minutes.

MEANWHILE, TOSS the apples and scallions in the remaining ¼ cup of olive oil. Add the bacon, garlic, sage, and rosemary and toss to combine. After the roast has cooked for 30 minutes at 350°F, add the apple mixture to the roasting pan and continue roasting for 1 hour more, or until an instant-read thermometer inserted directly into the end of each roast reaches 140°F. Remove the roast from the oven and transfer to a cutting board. (Leave the oven on.) Cover the meat with a piece of foil, tenting it so it sits loosely on the meat, and let rest for 20 minutes.

MEANWHILE, ADD THE BUTTER, cabbage, and thyme to the roasting pan. Toss to coat, then return the pan to the oven and roast until the cabbage is wilted and the onions and apples are tender, about 10 minutes. Transfer the cabbage mixture to a large platter and set aside.

POUR OFF ALL but 1 tablespoon of the fat from the pan and place the pan on the stovetop over medium heat. Add the cider and lemon juice, scraping up any bits from the bottom of the pan with a wooden spoon. Bring to a boil, reduce the heat to medium-low, and cook until the sauce coats the back of the wooden spoon.

CARVE THE PORK, cutting between the ribs, and arrange on top of the cabbage mixture. Drizzle the cider sauce over the pork and cabbage and serve.

---

chef tip: don't forget the fond

Fond, the French word for "base," refers to the brown carmelized bits of meat and vegetables stuck to the bottom of the pan after cooking. Scrape the bits with a wooden spoon, and add some stock, wine, or water to loosen them, then cook your vegetables in this flavorful sauce. However, if the fond is burnt, you have no choice but to discard, as it will impart a bitter flavor to your sauce or vegetables.

Steak Pizzaiola

Every once in a great while, my dad would commandeer the kitchen on Sundays. This was his signature dish, a favorite from his native Naples named for the pizza makers whose wives used their sauces to dress a nicely seared shell steak. I always knew fall had officially arrived when my mother broke out the jars of tomato sauce we put up at the end of the summer for this dish.

Swabbing up the sauce with crusty bread is mandatory, no matter how unglamorous it seems. It's a casual dish and should be enjoyed without judgment!

SERVES 4 TO 6

4–6 (8-ounce) shell steaks

Salt and freshly ground black pepper

5 tablespoons extra-virgin olive oil

4 garlic cloves, peeled and crushed

1 (28-ounce) can whole tomatoes

4 teaspoons dried oregano

Fresh oregano or flat-leaf parsley, for garnish

SEASON THE STEAKS on both sides with salt and pepper. Heat 3 tablespoons of the oil in a large skillet over medium-high heat until hot but not smoking. Sear the steaks on each side, in batches if necessary, until very deep brown, about 3 minutes. Transfer the steaks to a plate and set aside.

DRAIN THE FAT FROM THE PAN. Add the remaining 2 tablespoons of olive oil and heat until hot. Add the garlic, and sauté until golden, about 1 minute. Add the tomatoes, crushing them with your hands, and season with salt and pepper. Cook about 15 minutes, until the sauce thickens. Return the steaks and any accumulated juices to the pan, add the oregano, cover, and cook to the desired doneness (about 4 minutes for medium-rare).

PLACE EACH STEAK on a plate and spoon a bit of sauce on top. Garnish with the herbs, and serve warm.

FORMAL
FALL
DINNER

My birthday falls in September and these days, I prefer to celebrate with a few special people—and throw the party myself.

SETTING THE SCENE

I TAKE MY COLOR PALETTE cues from the season and then inject a little glamour to mark the occasion. I set the table using two of my favorite colors, silver and purple, and chose to wear a turquoise dress to continue the jewel-toned theme. For formal dinners, pull out the chargers—they frame the dinner plate so beautifully and immediately set the tone; this isn't a weekday meal....The gleam of the plates is enough bling for this kind of party , and makes a great foil for colorful glassware and linens. Keep the flowers simple and elegant; I like a few stems of magenta Phalenopsis orchids arranged in a pair of slightly different purple glass vases. The flowers are so beautiful, they need no arranging, which is the point! Pink orchids or gardenia blossoms floating in water are also beautiful.

WHAT TO SERVE

menu

PEAR AND CINNAMON COMPOTE WITH A SELECTION OF CHEESES, page 34

GORGONZOLA DOLCE, BACON, AND ONION CROSTINI, page 137

GENNARO'S BLACK KALE SALAD WITH CURRANTS, page 74

HALIBUT IN PHYLLO WITH PORCINI, SPINACH, AND FETA, page 161

COCONUT CAKE, page 212

WHAT TO POUR

FOR MY BIRTHDAY, I chose a wine producer from the Campagna region, where my father was born. I had the good fortune to visit the Feudi di San Gregorio winery and was immediately enchanted with their wine. With this as a starting point, I chose wines from the same producer so that my guests could enjoy and get to know the grape varietals from Naples. Whether or not you're entertaining for a special occasion, choose a wine that has some kind of meaning (and is, of course, appropriate with the menu), either to a special guest or because it recalls a memory of a visit to a particular country or region. Hard alcohol, if served at all, should come after the meal. A stiff drink before dinner deadens the palate (and often has the unfortunate effect of getting some guests tipsy).

PEAR AND CINNAMON COMPOTE WITH A SELECTION OF CHEESES; GORGONZOLA DOLCE, BACON, AND ONION CROSTINI: Greco Brut from Feudi di San Gregorio. Always start with bubbles; this brut's minerality is a perfect match for the pungent cheeses.

GENNARO'S BLACK KALE SALAD : Falanghina Del Sannio by Feudi di San Gregorio; the acidity holds up nicely to the garlicky dressing

HALIBUT IN PHYLLO WITH PORCINI, SPINACH, AND FETA: Serpico by Feudi di San Gregorio. Halibut is a fatty fish, and red wine pairs well with the richness of this dish.

COCONUT CAKE: Privilegio, a light, amber dessert wine

 **WHAT TO PLAY**

THE MUSIC FOR A SIT-DOWN dinner should vary in type and tempo over the course of the evening. Turn up the volume a bit as guests arrive and eat hors d'oeuvres, then turn it down a bit when everyone is seated at the table—you don't want your guests to have to shout to be heard. As the night winds down, turn the volume back up again and who knows, maybe some dancing will follow. On my playlist: Dave Matthews, Maroon 5, Beyonce, and Mary J. Blige. Shy away from anything too extreme; I'm a huge fan of 100-year-old Neapolitan love songs, but I only play them when my family comes for dinner! Well, I do play them while I'm cooking before my guests arrive!!

WHAT TO WEAR

I'M A BIG FAN OF DRESSES (the fewer moving parts, the better, I say!), and while a traditional cocktail dress may be a bit over-the-top for the occasion, it can be tamed by pairing it with boots and wearing your hair very casually. You could also go for a cigarette skirt with a dramatic top and heels. Just remember to balance the bling. One statement piece is enough.

chapter five

VEGE-
TABLES
and # SIDE
DISHES

Winter
Spinach and Gruyère Soufflés
Braised Broccoli Rabe with Olives and Red-Pepper Flakes
"Fried" Cauliflower
Roasted Root Vegetables

Spring
Pan-Sizzled Radicchio with Pancetta and Thyme
Roasted Asparagus with Parmigiano-Reggiano
Quinoa, Tabbouleh-Style
Pan-Fried New Potatoes with Chorizo

Summer
Tomato Gratin
Warm Potatoes with Arugula and Fresh Herbs
Fresh Fennel on Ice
French Beans with Garlic and Extra-Virgin Olive Oil

Fall
Roasted Brussels Sprouts with Walnuts and Pomegranates
Pan-Fried Italian Greens
Potato and Wild Mushroom Gratin
Braised Chestnuts with Lemon and Sage

It's the belt that makes the dress, the buttons that make the coat. And when it comes to putting a menu together, it's the side dishes that make the meal. Think about it. When you order in a restaurant, what drives you to choose the hamachi over the roasted half chicken? If you're anything like me, it's not the fish, chicken, or meat but the intriguing greens, potatoes, vegetables, and purees that go with them. I look at the side dishes first, and apparently I'm not the only one: In my years as a restaurateur, I've learned that nothing else on the menu gets customers to come back to the restaurant quite like a compelling mix of side dishes. At Mia Dona, it's quite common for a guest to make a meal of braised broccoli rabe with red-pepper flakes, polenta, and Brussels sprouts or to skip over the appetizers and choose a sautéed green to eat *before* dinner instead.

My point is, don't push side dishes off to the side. In Italy, sautéed or braised seasonal greens are invariably part of a meal. They're so simple and straightforward, yet a perfectly cooked mound of escarole or treviso has the power to make you look like a culinary giant. Of course, they should be noteworthy not only for their fine execution, but for their clever presentation, too. One of the easiest ways to draw attention to a delicious gratin is to miniaturize it. At my restaurants, the chefs perform a sleight of hand by making the tomato gratin in large batches, then spooning some into a warmed mini casserole dish for an individual order. Try the individual approach with soufflés. Rather than make one large one, divide the egg mixture into small ramekins—you'll be surprised how much mileage you get out of putting a tiny towering soufflé on each guest's plate.

Cooking with the seasons is in my DNA, but I admit it's difficult to stay true when you can buy asparagus in October and tomatoes in January. If there's one thing you should be rigid about, though, it's buying vegetables in season, preferably at their peak and from a green market. This is key, because the quality of your produce makes all the difference.

donatella do's for sides

- Invest in cute side containers—a great way to introduce a pop of color. Le Creuset in porcelain comes in great colors and is gorgeous and affordable.

- Buy in season; shop with your eyes as well. Tomato gratin comes alive when you buy different colors and varietals of tomatoes.

- Be careful with extra-virgin olive oil. You don't want delicious sides to become overly greasy.

- If you are serving a starchy side, such as a grain or potato dish, choose lighter green (spinach, asparagus, broccoli rabe) rather than a starchy one like beans or peas.

Spinach and Gruyère Soufflés

Soufflés aren't hard to make, and they are always so impressive! I love creamed spinach, but I never feel quite right serving it to guests. My answer—and the couture solution—is to transform creamed spinach into fluffy individual soufflés. Folding the egg whites into the egg mix properly is the key to lofty soufflés. The drama quotient is high, the stress level low, and your cooking savvy will seem off the charts. Serve these with the filet mignon (page 136). (See photo page 172.)

SERVES 6

YOU'LL NEED:
six 8-ounce ramekins, electric mixer

¾ cup (1½ sticks) unsalted butter, melted

¼ pound Gruyère, grated, plus more for dusting the ramekins

¼ cup all-purpose flour

1½ cups milk

4 large eggs, separated

6 ounces fresh spinach, washed, steamed, squeezed dry, and finely chopped

⅛ teaspoon freshly grated nutmeg

Kosher salt and freshly ground black pepper to taste

PREHEAT THE OVEN to 375°F with a baking sheet on a rack in the middle of the oven. Brush the insides of six 8-ounce ramekins with a little of the melted butter followed by a dusting of Gruyère.

PUT THE REMAINING MELTED BUTTER in a medium saucepan over medium heat. When it foams, reduce the heat and gradually add the flour, stirring until there is no trace of flour left in the mixture, about 3 minutes. Whisk in the milk in a thin stream and cook, stirring until the mixture thickens to the consistency of a heavy cream. Turn off the heat and whisk in the egg yolks until incorporated. Stir in the spinach and ¼ pound Gruyère and season with the nutmeg, and salt and pepper. Set aside.

BEAT THE EGG WHITES in a clean bowl with an electric mixer until stiff but not dry. Stir one-quarter of the egg whites into the spinach mixture to lighten it. Fold the remaining egg whites into the spinach mixture.

DIVIDE THE MIXTURE evenly among the ramekins, filling them to just below the rim. Run your finger around the inside rim of the each ramekin to make a groove in the mixture.

BAKE ABOUT 20 TO 25 MINUTES, until risen and golden brown on top. Serve immediately.

Braised Broccoli Rabe with Olives and Red-Pepper Flakes

I crave broccoli rabe the way some people crave chocolate. Call it genetic, but the truth is that I only came to love this quintessentially Italian vegetable in my 20s—as a child I found it too bitter. Braising the rabe, as I do here, tames its bitterness just enough to make it addictive. It's a perfect side dish on its own; toss it with sautéed sweet Italian sausage to make it a meal.

SERVES 4 TO 6

2 pounds broccoli rabe, trimmed of tough outer leaves and stem ends and thoroughly rinsed

½ cup extra-virgin olive oil

3 garlic cloves, thinly sliced

½ teaspoon red-pepper flakes

½ cup kalamata olives, pitted and quartered

COMBINE THE BROCCOLI RABE, olive oil, garlic, red-pepper flakes, and 2 cups of water in a pot. Cook, uncovered, over medium heat, stirring occasionally, until the broccoli rabe is fork tender, about 20 minutes. Toss with the olives and serve.

When I was young, my mom used to make me drink the water that was left over from broccoli rabe or another wild green like dandelion or escarole whenever I wasn't feeling well. I hated it then, but how things change. Recently, when my mom helped me develop the menu for Mia Dona, I was feeling under the weather. Guess what she made me drink? I protested that I wasn't eight anymore, but she insisted and, much to my surprise, it immediately revived me and tasted delicious!

"Fried" Cauliflower

My dear friend and Italian cooking authority Arthur Schwartz grew up in an Italian neighborhood (I, on the other hand, grew up in a predominantly Jewish neighborhood) and knows more about Italian food than most Italians I know. Whenever he is testing recipes for his cookbooks, he gathers his friends around for a tasting. The last meal was one of his best: pasta with pumpkin, swordfish with caponata, and this delectable cauliflower dish. If, like many people, you think cauliflower is bland, this will definitely change your mind and those of fellow detractors. Serve with the Tilapia Oreganata (page 138) or Scampi Ribelli (page 137).

SERVES 4 TO 6

1 head cauliflower, cored, broken into small florets (about 4 cups), washed, and well drained

3 large eggs, beaten

2 tablespoons heavy cream

½ cup grated Parmigiano-Reggiano or Grana Padano

4 tablespoons finely chopped fresh parsley

Kosher salt and freshly ground black pepper

2 tablespoons extra-virgin olive oil

BRING A LARGE POT of salted water to a rolling boil over high heat. Plunge the cauliflower into the water and cook for 2 minutes. Drain in a colander and run under cold water to cool cauliflower quickly. Set aside.

WHISK TOGETHER the eggs and heavy cream in a large bowl. Add the Parmigiano, 2 tablespoons of the parsley, and salt and pepper. Add the cauliflower to the egg mixture, gently turning the florets so that the egg mixture seeps into the crevices.

HEAT THE OLIVE OIL in a large nonstick skillet over medium heat. When the pan is hot enough to cook a drop of egg, give the cauliflower a final toss in the egg mixture. Transfer the cauliflower to the hot skillet using a slotted spoon. Drizzle the remaining egg mixture over the florets. When the egg begins to set, about 2 minutes, turn the cauliflower pieces using tongs. Cook the florets until lightly browned on all sides, about 5 minutes total. Transfer to a serving platter, garnish with the remaining 2 tablespoons parsley, and serve warm or at room temperature.

Roasted Root Vegetables

Soaking apples in a little sweet vermouth reminds me of my father, who loved to drink a little of the fortified wine on the rocks with his friends after work. While I'm not one to sip vermouth, I do like to use it as an ingredient. Here it raises the bar on a humble dish of root vegetables. If serving this to guests, put some care into your knife skills. Beautiful, uniform cubes make this homey dish elegant.

SERVES 4 TO 6

⅓ cup dried apples, diced

¼ cup sweet vermouth or white wine

3 turnips, peeled and cut into ½" cubes

2 large sweet potatoes, peeled and cut into ½" chunks

3 parsnips, peeled and cut into ½" chunks

1 small onion, roughly chopped

2 tablespoons extra-virgin olive oil

½ teaspoon kosher salt

Freshly ground black pepper

Chopped flat-leaf parsley, for garnish

SOAK THE DRIED APPLES in the vermouth for 20 minutes.

PREHEAT THE OVEN to 500° F.

TOSS THE TURNIPS, sweet potatoes, parsnips, and onion with the olive oil, salt, and plenty of pepper. Spread the vegetables on a large rimmed baking sheet and roast for 12 minutes, turning once, until softened and golden. Toss with the apples and any remaining liquid and transfer to a rimmed platter. Garnish with the parsley and serve warm.

Pan-Sizzled Radicchio with Pancetta and Thyme

Most people are accustomed to eating radicchio raw, in a salad, but cooking it gently tempers the leaves' bitter edge and raises it to a whole new level of lusciousness. Combine the leaves with pancetta and thyme in a ridiculously simple sauté, and you come out of the kitchen looking like an innovator.

SERVES 4

2 teaspoons extra-virgin olive oil

1 ounce pancetta, cut into matchsticks

2 large heads radicchio, halved lengthwise, leaves separated

2 sprigs fresh thyme

2 tablespoons red wine vinegar

½ teaspoon kosher salt

Freshly ground black pepper

WARM THE OIL in a heavy skillet over medium-high heat. Add the pancetta and cook about 6 minutes, until the fat is rendered and the pancetta is golden. Add the radicchio and thyme and sauté over medium-low heat, turning occasionally, for 8 to 10 minutes, until wilted and browned on both sides. Swirl in the vinegar, salt, and plenty of pepper, and remove from the heat. Serve warm or at room temperature.

Roasted Asparagus with Parmigiano-Reggiano

When I first started to entertain, this was the only side dish I would make. It was such a hit the first time (and the following dozen times after that) that I felt no compulsion to break up with a good thing. To up the elegance factor, go for the slenderest spears, and be generous with the Parmigiano and butter.

SERVES 4 TO 6

1½ pounds medium asparagus

2 tablespoons low-sodium chicken or vegetable broth

1 tablespoon white wine or vermouth

½ teaspoon kosher salt

Freshly ground black pepper

1 tablespoon unsalted butter, cut into pieces

1 cup grated Parmigiano-Reggiano

PREHEAT THE OVEN to 375°F.

SNAP OFF the woody ends of the asparagus and peel the bottom 2" of each stalk.

COMBINE THE ASPARAGUS, broth, wine, salt, and plenty of pepper in a small baking dish. Cover with aluminum foil and bake for 20 minutes. Remove the foil and sprinkle the butter and Parmigiano evenly over the asparagus. Bake, uncovered, for 5 minutes more, until the cheese is melted and golden. Serve warm.

Quinoa, Tabbouleh-Style

I was never much of a fan of tabbouleh—until I replaced the heavier, denser bulgur with delicate quinoa. The difference is amazing. This is a perfect combination of textures, with crisp vegetables studding the soft grains. Serve it with any grilled fish. By the way, quinoa is the perfect grain for those watching their carbs, as it is high in protein.

SERVES 4 TO 6

2 cups vegetables broth or water

Kosher salt

1 cup quinoa, rinsed

¼ cup extra-virgin olive oil plus more if needed

2 garlic cloves, smashed and very finely chopped

2 tablespoons fresh lemon juice plus more if needed

Freshly ground black pepper

4 large radishes, quartered lengthwise and sliced

3 ripe plum tomatoes, cored, seeded, and diced

½ English cucumber, seeded and diced

4 scallions, white and green parts, finely chopped

½ cup finely chopped flat-leaf parsley plus sprigs for garnish

BRING THE VEGETABLE BROTH to a simmer in a small saucepan, then add ¼ teaspoon salt (if using water, add ½ teaspoon salt). Stir in the quinoa and simmer, covered, until all the liquid has been absorbed and the grains are partially translucent, about 15 to 20 minutes. Transfer to a bowl and add the olive oil, garlic, lemon juice, another ½ teaspoon salt, and plenty of pepper. Toss, then refrigerate for at least 1 hour and up to 4 hours.

FLUFF THE QUINOA with a fork. Fold in the radishes, tomatoes, cucumber, scallions, and chopped parsley. Season with salt and pepper and more olive oil and lemon juice to taste. Garnish with the parsley sprigs.

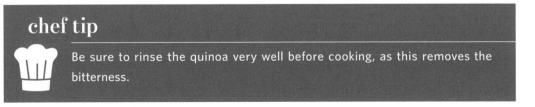

chef tip

Be sure to rinse the quinoa very well before cooking, as this removes the bitterness.

Pan-Fried New Potatoes with Chorizo

A little advice: Always have a link of chorizo on hand. I slice it up and put it in my omelet or on top of rice, and I sauté thin slices in a little copper pan and serve them straight from the stove as an hors d'oeuvres. Chorizo's bold flavor wakes up anything. Here, I toss it with tender-skinned new potatoes, a dish happily eaten as a main course when I'm cooking to suit myself. For guests, I partner it with the Cherry Tomato, Mint, Asparagus, and Gruyère Frittata (page 143). The recipe takes some time, almost none of which requires attention from you, so just start cooking before you begin the rest of your menu. The recipe can be doubled but you'll need 2 large skillets.

SERVES 4

2 tablespoons olive oil

1 small white or yellow onion, halved lengthwise and very thinly sliced

3–4 ounces cured chorizo, sliced about ⅓" thick

1 pound small red potatoes, washed, dried, and sliced ⅛" thick

3 garlic cloves, thinly sliced

2–3 sprigs fresh thyme

1 fresh bay leaf or 2 dried

Kosher salt and freshly ground black pepper

1 tablespoon finely chopped fresh herbs, such as flat-leaf parsley, dill, or chives

HEAT THE OIL IN A 12" SKILLET or sauté pan with a tight-fitting lid over medium heat. Add the onion and chorizo and cook, stirring occasionally, for about 10 minutes, until onion is wilted and slightly golden.

ADD THE POTATOES, garlic, thyme, and bay leaf and season with salt and pepper. Toss to coat all the ingredients with the fat and seasonings.

SPREAD IN AN EVEN LAYER, cover the pan, and cook very gently for 30 to 35 minutes, turning the potatoes over with a spatula two or three times. When the potatoes are fork-tender but not falling apart, remove the remains of the thyme sprigs and the bay leaf.

SPRINKLE THE CHOPPED HERBS all over and serve hot.

Tomato Gratin

I love tomatoes in any form, save for one: I never want them (and you should never serve them!) stuffed with rice and tuna, country-club style. Ripe, ripe tomato slices baked into a gratin with a little olive oil, basil, bread crumbs and Parmigiano-Reggiano, on the other hand, gives the summer tomato its due. It's an exquisite dish and exquisitely easy to pull together. In fact, you can prepare it ahead of time and warm it just before serving. Although they can overlap slightly, the tomatoes should essentially bake in a single layer, so make sure you have a large shallow dish, or use 2 small ones. If you have access to heirloom tomatoes, use them. The visual impact, not to mention the flavor, is beyond compare.

SERVES 4 TO 6

YOU'LL NEED: gratin dish or earthenware casserole

3 large, ripe tomatoes (preferably an heirloom variety), cored and sliced ½" thick

Kosher salt and freshly ground black pepper

4 tablespoons roughly chopped basil leaves

3 tablespoons extra-virgin olive oil

3 garlic cloves, very finely chopped

1 cup coarse, fresh bread crumbs, preferably made from sourdough bread

⅓ cup finely grated Parmigiano-Reggiano

PLACE THE TOMATO SLICES between 2 paper towels and let stand for 45 minutes to 1 hour. This will remove some of the liquid and keep the gratin from being soggy.

PREHEAT THE OVEN to 500°F with a rack in the center position. Brush a large, shallow gratin dish or earthenware casserole with a little olive oil.

ARRANGE THE TOMATO SLICES only just slightly overlapping in the dish. Season lightly with salt and pepper and scatter half the basil over the top.

HEAT THE OLIVE OIL in a small skillet over medium-high heat. Add the garlic and sauté only until the aroma is released, about 45 seconds. Remove from the heat and stir in the bread crumbs and a pinch of salt and pepper. Scatter the bread crumb mixture over the tomatoes and top with the Parmigiano.

BAKE FOR ABOUT 15 MINUTES, until the crumbs are golden. If desired, let stand for up to 1 hour and reheat in a low oven for 5 to 10 minutes before serving. Just before serving, garnish with the remaining 2 tablespoons of basil.

Warm Potatoes with Arugula and Fresh Herbs

If you can find baby arugula for this dish, use it. It's milder than the full-grown variety, but still retains a distinctive tang. It's perfect paired with the Straccetti (page 151), Grilled Whole Branzino (page 153), or Salmon in Cartoccio (page 154).

SERVES 4 TO 6

1¼ pounds small red potatoes, scrubbed and halved

2 tablespoons extra-virgin olive oil

1 teaspoon kosher salt

Freshly ground black pepper

½ cup roughly chopped baby arugula

1 clove garlic, very finely chopped

2 tablespoons roughly chopped fresh dill and/or mint

WARM AN OVENPROOF SERVING BOWL in a low oven.

STEAM THE POTATOES over simmering water for 13 to 14 minutes, until nearly tender. Turn them out into the warm bowl and add the olive oil, salt, and plenty of pepper. Toss to coat with the oil. Add the arugula, garlic, and dill to the bowl and toss again. Serve warm.

Fresh Fennel on Ice

One ingredient, a little chopping, no cooking, and guests will be in awe. I served this to my friend Stephen Scoble, creative director of *Food, and Wine,* as part of a Puglian dinner I prepared, and more than any other it was the dish that got people talking. Grabbing the slivers right from a trifle dish created a great sense of communal casualness. It's perfect right after the main course or just before serving cheese and fruit because it aids digestion. If you have a footed trifle bowl, use it!

SERVES 4 TO 6

3 small fennel bulbs, stalks discarded

Selection of artisanal salts, for dipping

HALVE THE FENNEL BULBS lengthwise and cut out the cores. Cut each half into thirds or quarters, depending on its size. Arrange the fennel chunks in a bowl filled with crushed ice and water. Place individual salts in small bowls. Let guests help themselves.

French Beans with Garlic and Extra-Virgin Olive Oil

I always knew when the seasons had officially changed based on what my mother put on the dinner table. This dish marked the official start of spring, and it showed up on our plates regularly until summer arrived. When I first lived on my own, I spent a lot of time on the phone with my mother, trying to pin her down on the details of my favorite recipes. This was one of the ones she shared, but I couldn't understand why my beans didn't taste like hers. Then I realized that I shouldn't use frozen ones! The long and short of it is, use fresh, tender, farm-stand (if at all possible) green beans. Another tip from my mom: The longer the cooked beans sit at room temperature, the better they taste.

SERVES 4 TO 6

6 garlic cloves, smashed and finely chopped

3 tablespoons extra-virgin olive oil

Kosher salt and freshly ground black pepper

1¼ pounds fresh French or string beans, trimmed

2 tablespoons coarsely chopped flat-leafed parsley or fresh dill

BRING A LARGE POT of water to a rolling boil for the beans. Combine the garlic, oil, ¼ teaspoon salt, and plenty of pepper in a large bowl.

ADD A LARGE PINCH of salt to the boiling water and cook the beans for 4 to 6 minutes (4 minutes for very tiny French beans; 6 minutes for string beans). Immediately drain in a colander and dump into the bowl with the garlic. Toss with tongs until all the beans are well coated and the garlic releases its aroma. Add the parsley and toss again. Serve at room temperature.

Roasted Brussels Sprouts with Walnuts and Pomegranates

I made a classic holiday dish like Brussels sprouts glamorous by adding ruby red pomegranate seeds. Spare yourself the job of plucking the seeds from the fruit—it's a thankless task better left to the produce department. They are usually packed in containers near the prepared fresh fruit.

SERVES 4 TO 6

1 quart small Brussels sprouts, trimmed of outer leaves and halved through the stem end

8 tablespoons extra-virgin olive oil

Kosher salt and freshly ground black pepper

Juice of 2 lemons

1 cup walnuts, toasted (below)

½ cup fresh pomegranate seeds

2 ounces pecorino cheese shaved with a vegetable peeler

PREHEAT THE OVEN to 450°F.

COMBINE THE BRUSSELS SPROUTS and 3 tablespoons of the olive oil in a large bowl and toss to coat. Season with salt and pepper. Transfer to a rimmed baking sheet and roast until fork tender and some of the outer leaves are crunchy, about 20 minutes. Set aside to cool.

MEANWHILE, WHISK TOGETHER the remaining 5 tablespoons of olive oil and the lemon juice in a small bowl. Toss the sprouts in a large bowl with the walnuts and pomegranate seeds. Transfer to a serving platter. Season with salt and pepper and drizzle with the vinaigrette. Sprinkle with the pecorino and serve.

chef tip: how to toast nuts

Preheat the oven to 350°F. Spread the nuts on a small baking sheet or in an ovenproof skillet. Toast until golden and fragrant, 5 to 10 minutes depending on the nut, turning once.

Pan-Fried Italian Greens

I cannot recall a single meal at which my mother failed to serve some kind of cooked green: escarole, chicory, dandelion greens. She always prepares them the same way—sautéed in olive oil and garlic—but when you're cooking to impress, you really should embellish. Pine nuts and golden raisins add a savory and sweet touch, with very little effort on your part. I use escarole here, but you could substitute the outer, green parts of a head of curly endive (also known as frisée) and save the pale inner hearts for a raw salad.

SERVES 4 TO 6

2 tablespoons golden raisins

2 medium heads escarole, brown or wilted leaves trimmed away

¼ cup extra-virgin olive oil

3 large garlic cloves, very finely chopped

2 tablespoons pine nuts, toasted (page 49)

⅓ cup pitted Kalamata olives, quartered

¼–½ teaspoon red-pepper flakes

Kosher salt and freshly ground black pepper

COVER THE RAISINS with warm water and soak for 20 minutes. Rinse the escarole well and shake once or twice in a colander. Slice crosswise into 1½" strips. Drain the raisins.

COMBINE THE OLIVE OIL, garlic, and slightly wet escarole in a large skillet or sauté pan. Cook over medium-low heat for 5 minutes, then throw in the raisins, pine nuts, olives, and pepper flakes. Cook for 3 to 5 minutes more, until the escarole is tender but still nice and green. Season to taste with salt (the olives are salty, so use caution) and pepper.

chef tip

Chefs use stainless steel ring molds, but you can pack a ½-cup stainless steel measuring cup to the rim with greens, then flip it onto the plate for an architectural presentation of the greens.

Potato and Wild Mushroom Gratin

Excellent ingredients, layered and baked, don't require intense attention or focus and taste even better if made ahead. This gratin is perfect for the Thanksgiving table, whether you are hosting dinner or are asked to bring a dish to a party. Serve it straight from the oven or for more formal occasions, cut it into wedges.

SERVES 4 TO 6

1½ pounds white or red rose potatoes, peeled

1 tablespoon extra-virgin olive oil plus extra for drizzling

1 tablespoon unsalted butter

1 large onion, sliced thinly

5 ounces wild mushrooms (shiitake, oyster, and/or chanterelle), cleaned and thinly sliced

½ teaspoon kosher salt

Freshly ground black pepper

2 garlic cloves, very finely chopped

1½ teaspoons chopped fresh marjoram

½ teaspoon finely chopped fresh thyme

¼ teaspoon dried Greek oregano

1¼ cups low-sodium chicken broth

SLICE THE POTATOES very thinly. As you slice, place them in a large bowl of cold water and soak for 10 minutes.

HEAT 1 TABLESPOON OF THE OLIVE OIL and butter in a large, heavy skillet over medium-low heat. Add the onion and mushrooms and sauté until softened. Season with ¼ teaspoon of the salt and plenty of pepper. Remove from the heat.

PREHEAT THE OVEN to 425°F with the rack in the lower third of the oven.

COMBINE THE GARLIC, marjoram, thyme, oregano, remaining ¼ teaspoon salt, and more pepper. Brush a large oval or rectangular baking dish with a little olive oil. Drain the potatoes and pat them dry with paper towels. Make 1 layer of sliced potatoes, overlapping. Distribute about one-quarter of the mushroom mixture over the potatoes, then scatter a little of the garlic-herb mixture over the top and drizzle with about 2 teaspoons of olive oil. Continue layering the remaining potatoes, mushrooms, garlic mixture, and olive oil, finishing with a layer of the herb mixture and a drizzle of olive oil. Pour the chicken broth around the edges of the dish and cover with foil.

BAKE UNTIL THE POTATOES ARE PERFECTLY TENDER when pierced with a fork, about 30 minutes. Remove the foil and bake for 10 to 15 minutes more to cook off the excess liquid, if necessary. Let stand for 10 to 15 minutes, and slice into wedges.

Braised Chestnuts with Lemon and Sage

Christmastime was the only time of year my mother ever roasted chestnuts and inevitably, in the frenzy of friends and family coming and going all day, she would forget to watch them and they'd end up burned. Now I buy them cooked and peeled in vacuum-packed jars at specialty food stores and can enjoy them all year long. Discard any broken chestnuts and toss them delicately so they stay whole. Serve these with the Roasted Rack of Pork (page 162).

SERVES 4 TO 6

YOU'LL NEED:
citrus stripper

14–16 ounces cooked and peeled chestnuts

2 tablespoons butter

2 teaspoons dark or light brown sugar

½ teaspoon kosher salt

1 large sprig fresh sage plus 10–15 extra sage leaves for garnish, optional

1 lemon, peel removed in long strands with a citrus stripper

Canola oil for frying sage (optional)

COMBINE THE CHESTNUTS, butter, brown sugar, salt, sage sprig, and ⅓ cup of water in a large skillet. Bring to a simmer over medium-high heat and cook, uncovered, tossing frequently, until the water has evaporated, the butter begins to sizzle, and the chestnuts begin to brown, 5 to 8 minutes. Continue cooking, shaking the pan to toss the chestnuts back and forth, until they are nicely caramelized. Remove the sage sprig and, if you are not adding sage leaves for garnish, stir in the lemon zest and serve warm.

TO FRY WHOLE SAGE LEAVES: Be sure the leaves are completely dry. Fry in ¼" very hot oil just until crisp, 1 to 2 minutes. Add the lemon zest to the pan and fry 30 seconds to 1 minute more. Scatter all over chestnuts.

donatella clicks

If you can't find cooked and peeled chestnuts in vacuum-packed jars in your local specialty food store, D'Artagnan (www.dartagnan.com) will ship them to you, along with a wide variety of classic French specialties.

chapter six

DESSERTS

Winter

Prosecco Floats

Nutella Hot Chocolate

White Chocolate Risotto

Almost Flourless Chocolate Cake

Spring

Panna Cotta with Berries and Anise Brittle

Lemon Ricotta Fritters

Coconut Cake

Zia Donata's Ricotta Cheesecake

Summer

Cannolis

Sparkling Watermelon with Yogurt Cream and Mint

Plum Crostata

Cotton Candy

Strawberry Semifreddo

Fall

Rice Pudding

Pumpkin Bread Pudding

Roasted Pears with Chocolate Sauce and Amaretti

Easy Chocolate Sauce

Ice Wine Jell-O Shots

My favorite dessert, without exception, is coconut cake. The neighborhood I grew up in, Astoria, Queens, was home to Walken's Bakery, where, quite possibly, the world's best version was made. This storied bake shop—where actor Christopher Walken, son of the owners, ran the cash register—closed several years ago, but up until the day the doors were locked for good, a photo of my coconut birthday cake, inscribed with my name, hung on the wall. When we moved to Long Island, my mother's best friend, Alice, brought my beloved cake every year on my birthday. Fast-forward a few decades and that coconut cake has stayed with me: I insisted that one inspired by Walken's—towering golden cake layers covered in white frosting and fresh coconut—be on the menu at one of my first restaurants. (It's also in this chapter.)

My passion for coconut cake is close to an obsession, but generally Italians only go for such elaborate confections on holidays and for celebrations. The rest of the time, fresh fruit, usually served whole and in a bowl or on a platter, is set out for dessert. Seasonal fruit tossed in a liqueur is as elaborate as it usually gets.

I have to say that this tradition used to suit me nicely. Watermelon chunks tossed in sambuca made me look like a rock star, as did floating tiny scoops of sorbet in a glass of prosecco. But when I began entertaining in earnest, I realized that, as enticing as these boozy desserts were, guests were often looking for something they could really sink their sweet tooth into. So I looked to the celebration desserts of Italy, and recast them to reflect my modern sensibility (and my impatience with precise measurements!). I lightened up the zeppoles (traditional fried doughnuts) by using fresh ricotta and lemon, and, rather than swabbing Nutella onto bread, I stirred it into hot chocolate. As for Zia Donata's Cheesecake, the inclusion of heavy whipping cream makes it the most ethereal version you'll ever bake, as well as the easiest.

Of course, I couldn't ignore the classics—panna cotta, semifreddo, poached pears, plum crostata—all of which a cook should master to truly earn her cooking stripes. None requires elaborate techniques, equipment, or special ingredients. Frivolity, however, is a secret weapon, which is why you'll find suggestions for dusting a decadent chocolate cake with gold dust, sprinkling iridescent sanding sugar into a sparkling drink, and scattering colorful nonpareils on a cheesecake the way my aunt Isabella did. I've even included a "recipe" for cotton candy, inspired by the luminous cloud served at The Four Seasons in Manhattan as well as Anthos. That one does require you to buy a machine to make it, but that shouldn't stop you—the ethereal, snow-white clouds will define your dinner parties for years to come. I must give a special thanks to Zak Miller, executive pastry chef, for all his help with this section. I could not have done it without him!

donatella do's for desserts

- Keep some bling on hand for dessert adornment—sanding sugars, edible gold dust, gourmet marshmallows.

- Measure! More than ever with desserts. It's key, so follow my easy recipes to a T.

- Baking and dessert products are inherently inexpensive, and making desserts is infinitely cheaper than buying, so don't skimp on ingredients. It will make all the difference. Buy the best-quality butter, flour, sugar, and chocolate that you can afford.

Prosecco Floats

Who has time to think about dessert on New Year's Eve when there is champagne to buy and caviar and oysters to order? Here's my solution: one last glass of bubbly with a sparkling, sweet twist.

SERVES 4 TO 6

YOU'LL NEED:
melon baller

1 pint lemon sorbet or other flavor of your choice

1 bottle (750 ml) prosecco sparkling wine

4–6 lemon twists

Fresh mint leaves, for garnish

Iridescent sanding sugar or edible gold dust (optional)

SCOOP 3 SMALL BALLS of sorbet into each glass using a melon baller. Fill to within ½" of the rim with the prosecco. Garnish with a lemon twist and mint leaves and sprinkle a tiny pinch of sanding sugar into the glass.

donatella clicks

Some of the most gorgeous varieties of sanding sugar—opal, silver, iridescent, gold—are available at www.amazon.com. A nice assortment is also available at www.confectioneryhouse.com.

Nutella Hot Chocolate

Nutella, a hazelnut spread, is the peanut butter of the Italian pantry. Growing up, I ate it straight from the jar and, of course, between 2 slices of Wonder bread. (Try it on rustic Italian bread seasoned with a little sea salt for the world's easiest hors d'oeuvre or snack.) Every few years, New York is slammed with a major snowstorm. The whole city seems to shut down and most of us get an unexpected day off, which becomes a perfect opportunity to indulge in that most wintry of winter drinks, hot chocolate. Here's a version with an Italian twist.

SERVES 4 TO 6

2 cups whole milk

2 cups half-and-half

10 ounces bittersweet chocolate, chopped (I recommend Valrhona)

½ cup Nutella

Gourmet marshmallows, toasted if desired (optional, see Donatella Clicks)

COMBINE THE MILK and half-and-half in a saucepan and bring to a low boil. Remove from the heat and add the chocolate and Nutella. Whisk until the chocolate is melted and the ingredients are thoroughly combined. Cover to keep hot. If using marshmallows (and you should!), toast them, one at a time over a gas flame, turning until all sides are golden brown. Pour the hot chocolate into small coffee mugs, top with the marshmallows, and serve hot.

donatella clicks

Don't go for cheap supermarket marshmallows. Plush Puffs gourmet marshmallows come in a variety of flavors and are available in most major grocery stores and online at www.plushpuffs.com.

White Chocolate Risotto

During a competition I judged on *The Next Iron Chef*, the challenge was to make a dessert without sugar or butter. Chef John Besh made a bread pudding with white chocolate (which isn't chocolate at all, but cocoa butter). It was the best bread pudding I'd ever had. I created this dish based on his sly use of white chocolate, and the results are to die for.

To make the risotto ahead of time, you can stop cooking it after the second addition of milk and spread it on a large baking sheet to cool. When you are ready to serve, return it to the pot, add the remaining milk and stir over medium heat, then finish as below. Add a nice variety of dried fruits: Raisins, dried cranberries, and dried cherries may be left whole; apricots, plums, or pears should be diced into similar sized pieces. All of the rules for making a savory risotto apply (see page 93).

SERVES 4 TO 6

YOU'LL NEED: electric mixer, Microplane zester

1 cup heavy cream

6 ounces white chocolate, chopped plus some shards

1 cup assorted dried fruits, chopped

¾–1 cup white wine (optional)

1 tablespoon unsalted butter

½ cup arborio or Carnaroli rice

2½ cups whole milk, warmed

2 tablespoons sugar

1 vanilla bean, split, or ¼ teaspoon pure vanilla extract

Zest of ½ orange, removed with a zester or Microplane

Pinch of saffron threads

HEAT THE CREAM in a saucepan over medium heat just until it comes to a boil. Meanwhile, place the chocolate in a large heatproof bowl. Pour the hot cream over the top. Let stand for 1 minute, then whisk until smooth. Cool, cover, and chill in the refrigerator for at least 4 hours, or overnight.

SOAK THE DRIED FRUITS in warm water or the white wine. Whip the chilled white chocolate cream with an electric mixer until soft peaks form. Set aside.

MELT THE BUTTER in a large saucepan. Add the rice and cook for about 1 minute, stirring occasionally. Add ½ cup of milk, the sugar, vanilla, orange zest, and saffron and stir constantly over medium heat until most of the milk has been absorbed. Add another ½ cup of milk and stir. Repeat this process until all the milk has been absorbed, 18 to 20 minutes. Remove from the heat and fold in the whipped white chocolate cream; the risotto will be the consistency of oatmeal. Spoon into a bowl or glass. Drain the dried fruits and spoon them on top. Garnish each with a few white chocolate shards.

Almost Flourless Chocolate Cake

Every girl needs to know how to make a good chocolate cake; it's the little black dress of desserts. Dress it up with a dusting of confectioner's sugar for an afternoon get-together or give it a glamorous touch with edible gold powder for a dinner party (see page 116 for source). The success of this cake relies entirely on the quality of the chocolate you use, so buy the best you can afford. My preference is Valrhona. (See photo page 198.)

> **MAKES ONE 8"**
> **SINGLE-LAYER**
> **CAKE; SERVES**
> **6 TO 8**
>
> **YOU'LL NEED:**
> double boiler
> or stainless
> steel bowl,
> electric mixer,
> 8" springform
> pan

8 ounces top-quality bittersweet chocolate, coarsely chopped

1 cup (2 sticks) unsalted butter

1¼ cups sugar

4 large eggs

½ cup all-purpose flour

Confectioners' sugar or edible gold dust, for dusting

Mint leaves, for garnish

1 pint lemon, orange, or grapefruit sorbet

PREHEAT THE OVEN to 325°F. Coat an 8" springform pan with butter.

PUT THE CHOCOLATE in the top of a double boiler or in a stainless steel bowl placed over a saucepan one-quarter full of water. Melt the chocolate over medium-high heat, stirring frequently with a rubber spatula. Alternatively, put the chocolate in a microwave-safe bowl and melt in the microwave on medium power.

MEANWHILE, COMBINE the butter and sugar and beat with an electric mixer on medium-high speed until light and fluffy. Add the eggs one at a time, beating until incorporated after each addition. Add the melted chocolate and beat until combined. Add the flour and mix until just incorporated (don't overbeat!). Pour the batter into the pan and bake until the top forms a thin crust, 35 to 40 minutes. Cool the cake in the pan on a rack. When completely cooled, remove the sides from the pan, then use a long spatula to loosen cake from the pan bottom and slide onto a cake plate or stand. Dust with confectioners' sugar by tapping the sugar through a fine-mesh sieve. Garnish with the mint leaves and serve with a scoop of sorbet.

Panna Cotta with Berries and Anise Brittle

This is the Italian answer to crème brûlée. The crackle comes from an intriguing anise-flavored brittle. Even though it's relatively easy to make, panna cotta always seems to impress. You can make it even easier by buying good-quality gourmet brittle instead of making your own or by drizzling a little maple syrup (squeezed through a squeeze bottle) on the panna cotta and garnishing with candied walnuts. Once you master the basic recipe, change the add-ins based on the season. Put the panna cotta mixture into wine glasses or small ramekins with enough headroom so to allow room for the berries and anise brittle. Be precise with gelatin powder; too much and it's a rubbery mess.

SERVES 8

YOU'LL NEED:
eight 6-ounce ramekins or wineglasses

Panna Cotta

1 tablespoon plus 2 teaspoons powdered unflavored gelatin

2 cups whole milk

1 cup sugar

1 vanilla bean, split and seeds scraped away, or ¼ teaspoon vanilla extract

2 cups very cold heavy cream

Anise Brittle

1 tablespoon unsalted butter, at room tempurature

¼ cup sugar

2 tablespoons light corn syrup

¼ cup fennel seeds

¼ teaspoon baking soda

Fresh seasonal berries, for serving

TO MAKE THE PANNA COTTA: Put ¼ cup cold water in a small bowl. Sprinkle the gelatin over it and let it soak for 5 minutes, or until softened. Combine the milk, sugar, and vanilla bean halves in a large saucepan. Stir over medium-high heat until the sugar has dissolved, then bring to a gentle boil. Remove from the heat and let cool for 2 minutes. Stir in the gelatin mixture until dissolved. Stir in the cream and remove the pieces of vanilla bean. Cool to room temperature, then refrigerate for 30 minutes, or until the mixture begins to thicken.

POUR ½ CUP of the mixture into each of eight 6-ounce ramekins or glasses. Refrigerate for at least 2 hours, until set. If you plan to refrigerate overnight, cover each with plastic wrap.

TO MAKE THE ANISE BRITTLE: Line a baking sheet with foil and rub with the butter. Combine the sugar, corn syrup, and 2 tablespoons of water in a small, heavy saucepan. Heat over medium-high heat, stirring, until the sugar has dissolved. Then bring to a boil and simmer until the bubbles begin to break much more slowly. (Note: Molten sugar is *extremely* hot; handle it with care.) Shortly after that, the mixture will start to brown. Caramelize it to a light amber color—*not* dark brown. Remove from the heat and stir in the fennel seeds and

baking soda (the mixture will bubble up slowly and expand like a science experiment). Scoop it out onto the buttered foil with a spatula and spread thinly; it will continue bubbling for a few seconds. Cool completely, then chop the hard brittle into small, rough pieces.

TO SERVE, top each panna cotta with a few berries and scatter with the chopped brittle.

Lemon Ricotta Fritters

When I opened Bellini in the mid-1990s, I wanted to serve my grandmother's zeppoles—fried balls of dough dusted with sugar—with tiny pots of chocolate sauce for dipping. My dad insisted it wasn't elegant enough for a Midtown Manhattan restaurant, that it was too reminiscent of street food. He was wrong. The customers *looooved* it then (served with a tiny tub of warm chocolate sauce) and love it just as much in this iteration as it is currently served at Mia Dona. Serve these with Easy Chocolate Sauce (page 232) in individual butter warmers.

SERVES 4 TO 6

1 cup all-purpose flour

1½ teaspoons baking powder

¼ teaspoon salt

3 large eggs

3 tablespoons plus ½ cup sugar

½ pound fresh ricotta

2 tablespoons grated lemon zest

½ teaspoon vanilla extract

1 teaspoon ground cinnamon

3–4 cups vegetable oil, for deep-frying

SIFT TOGETHER the flour, baking powder, and salt in a bowl. Set aside. Whisk together the eggs and 3 tablespoons of the sugar in a large bowl. Add the ricotta, lemon zest, and vanilla and stir until just combined. Do not overmix. Gradually add the flour mixture to the ricotta mixture and stir until smooth. Combine the remaining ½ cup of sugar and the cinnamon in a small bowl. Set aside.

HEAT THE OIL in a medium saucepan over medium-high heat until hot and faint streaks appear on the bottom of the pan. Working in batches, carefully drop 1 tablespoon of dough at a time into the oil and fry, turning several times, until golden brown. Adjust the heat as needed to prevent the fritters from burning. Do not walk away from the pan while the fritters fry. Drain on paper towels or on a brown paper bag.

TOSS THE WARM FRITTERS in the cinnamon-sugar mixture, pile on a rimmed serving platter, and serve immediately.

Coconut Cake

I've been celebrating my birthday with a coconut cake ever since I can remember. If you learn to make one cake, make it this one. It's perfect not only for birthday parties, but wedding and baby showers, holidays, and anniversaries. Note that you need both coconut milk and sweetened cream of coconut (the coconut flavoring used in cocktails) for this recipe. A special thank-you to Gustavo Tzoc, former pastry chef at davidburke & donatella, for helping me perfect this recipe.

SERVES 8 TO 12

YOU'LL NEED:
two 9" round cake pans, electric mixer

Cake

6 large eggs

1½ cups (3 sticks) unsalted butter, at room temperature

2½ cups sugar

2½ cups all-purpose flour, sifted

1½ tablespoons baking powder

2 teaspoons salt

2⅔ cups coconut milk

1 tablespoon coconut rum

1 teaspoon vanilla extract

1 tablespoon cream of tartar

1 cup sweetened shredded coconut

Filling

2¼ cups sweetened shredded coconut

1¼ cups cream of coconut

4½ teaspoons powdered, unflavored gelatin

3 tablespoons pure vanilla extract

¼ cup milk

4 cups whipping cream

2 cups sweetened shredded coconut

Silver nonpareils, for garnish (optional)

TO MAKE THE CAKE: Preheat the oven to 350°F. Grease two 9" round cake pans with butter and coat with flour. Tap out the excess.

SEPARATE THE EGGS, placing the yolks in a medium bowl and the whites in a second medium bowl.

COMBINE THE BUTTER and 2 cups of the sugar in a medium bowl beat on medium speed with an electric mixer until the mixture is pale yellow and fluffy. Add the egg yolks, one at a time, beating until incorporated after each addition. Beat until the mixture comes together.

COMBINE THE FLOUR, baking powder and salt in a medium bowl. Stir together the coconut milk, coconut rum, and vanilla in a small bowl. With the mixer on slow speed, add the flour mixture and the milk mixtures to the butter mixture, adding them alternately in batches. When the batter is smooth, transfer it to a large, clean bowl and set aside.

WASH AND DRY THE BEATERS WELL. Combine the egg whites and cream of tartar in a clean bowl and beat on medium speed until soft peaks form. Add the remaining ½ cup of sugar in a slow stream and beat until the whites appear glossy.

FOLD ONE-THIRD of the egg whites into the batter, followed by one-third more, and then the remaining egg whites. Fold in the shredded coconut. Pour the batter into the cake pans and bake for 35 minutes, or until golden brown on top and a knife inserted in the middle comes out clean. Cool the cakes in the pans on a rack.

TO MAKE THE FILLING: Put the shredded coconut in a large bowl and set aside. Heat ½ cup of the cream of coconut in a small saucepan over medium heat until hot. Add the gelatin and the vanilla. Remove from the heat and stir in the remaining ¾ cup of cream of coconut. Add the mixture to the shredded coconut.

BEAT THE WHIPPING CREAM at medium speed until very soft peaks form. Fold the whipped cream into the shredded coconut mixture until incorporated. Cover and refrigerate for 30 minutes.

MEANWHILE, TOAST THE REMAINING coconut for garnish. Preheat the oven to 325°F. Spread the coconut in a single layer on a baking sheet. Bake for 12 to 15 minutes, or until the flakes are browned around the edges or, if preferred, until the entire flake is browned. Set aside to cool.

TO ASSEMBLE: When the cakes have cooled, remove them from the pans. Place 1 cake on a serving platter. Spoon half of the filling over the surface, top with a second layer, and spoon the remaining filling on the top and spread over the sides. Place in the freezer for at least 1 hour. Pat the toasted coconut all over the cake and garnish with the nonpareils, if desired, just before serving.

Zia Donata's Ricotta Cheesecake

Aunt Donata, my namesake and the best baker in the family, came to America right after I was born. I couldn't write a cookbook without paying homage to her, which is lucky for you because her cheesecake will blow your mind. I call it her magic cake, because it is deceptively light and fluffy. That's thanks to her secret: whipped cream. It's deceptively easy, too. Zia Donata essentially dumps all of the ingredients into a soup pot! All of my aunts dust every dessert with tiny multicolored non-pareils; it's a charming decoration on the top of this cake. For a more formal occasion, I opt for a caramelized sugar flourish (as shown here).

SERVES 6 TO 8

YOU'LL NEED: electric mixer, 9" springform pan

Cheesecake

8 large eggs

2 cups sugar

½ cup all-purpose flour, sifted

3 pounds fresh ricotta

½ cup heavy cream, whipped to soft peaks

Juice and grated zest of 1 lemon, juice strained

¾ teaspoon vanilla extract

¼ cup sweet liqueur such as limoncello or Strega

Topping (optional)

1 tablespoon confectioners' sugar

1 cup granulated sugar

PREHEAT THE OVEN to 350°F. Butter the bottom and sides of a 9" springform pan.

TO MAKE THE CHEESECAKE: Beat the eggs in a large bowl with an electric mixer until foamy and light yellow. Add the sugar and beat on medium speed until smooth. Add the flour and beat until incorporated. Add the ricotta and whipped cream and beat until smooth. Add the lemon juice, lemon zest, vanilla, and liqueur to the ricotta and stir gently until incorporated. Pour the mixture into the pan, place on a rimmed baking sheet, and bake for 1 hour 45 minutes or until a toothpick inserted in the center comes out clean. Turn off the oven and leave the cheesecake in it to settle for 10 minutes. Remove from the oven to cool completely. Dust the top of the cheesecake with confectioners' sugar (this will be the background for the caramel flourish).

TO MAKE THE DECORATIVE TOPPING: Line a baking sheet with wax paper. Put the granulated sugar in a saucepan over medium heat. Stir constantly as the sugar melts. It will bubble and begin to turn golden. When the liquid becomes deep golden, remove from the stove. Dip a metal spoon into the molten sugar and drizzle onto the wax paper, forming letters or designs. Let harden, then gently peel off the paper and arrange on the cheesecake. If making ahead, cover and refrigerate and bring to room temperature before serving.

Cannolis

Give me a cannoli and I'm in heaven. They may suggest old-Italian-pastry-shop quaintness, but it's all in the way you decorate and serve them. Look for good-quality shells and, most importantly, whip that cream! Rather than using primary colored candies on either end, opalescent nonpareils take them right out of the bakery case. My cream filling features Strega, an Italian digestif redolent of mint and fennel.

SERVES 6

YOU'LL NEED:
electric mixer

---

1 pound fresh ricotta, drained

¼ cup Strega or orange liqueur

1¼ cups confectioners' sugar

¼ teaspoon ground cinnamon

Grated zest of ½ orange

Pinch of salt

6 large cannoli shells or 12 small

Opalescent nonpareils

COMBINE THE RICOTTA, liqueur, sugar, cinnamon, orange zest, and salt in a bowl. Using a whisk or electric mixer, whisk on medium speed until the mixture is light and creamy, about 2 minutes.

SPOON THE CREAM into a resealable plastic bag. Snip off one of the corners. Squeeze the cream into the cannoli shells and sprinkle either end with the nonpareils.

donatella clicks

Vigo and Alessi (www.vigo-alessi.com) sells all manner of Italian products online, including cannoli shells in varying sizes. Believe it or not, you can also find them at www.amazon.com.

Sparkling Watermelon with Yogurt Cream and Mint

I have long felt that in white tablecloth establishments, it's important to have a little fun. And it turns out, my high-flying professional clientele agrees. When a server shows up at their table with cotton candy (page 222), all conversation turns to the cloud of spun sugar before them. The same is true of this dessert, which incorporates that explode-in-your-mouth phenomenon from childhood, Pop Rocks. They can make a crowd of snobby food lovers lose control and laugh out loud.

SERVES 6 TO 8

YOU'LL NEED:
electric mixer

Yogurt Cream

18 ounces full-fat plain Greek yogurt

¼ cup sugar

2 egg whites

¾ cup heavy cream

Juice of 1 lemon

Watermelon

1 small seedless watermelon, cut into 1" cubes

Maldon sea salt

Pop Rocks

¼ cup tiny mint leaves

TO MAKE THE YOGURT CREAM: Place the yogurt in a large bowl and set aside.

COMBINE THE SUGAR and egg whites in a medium bowl and beat with an electric mixer on medium speed until the mixture forms soft peaks, about the consistency of shaving cream. Fold the egg white mixture into the yogurt until no whites appear. Fold the heavy cream into the mixture until combined. Stir in the lemon juice.

TO ASSEMBLE: Place 5 pieces of the watermelon on a dessert plate. Spoon 2 tablespoons of the yogurt cream over them. Sprinkle with a pinch of sea salt. Top with a generous teaspoon of Pop Rocks and some mint slivers.

donatella clicks

Pop Rocks are as essential to my dessert pantry as salt and pepper are to my cooking staples. You can turn almost any ordinary dessert—especially the fruit and frozen variety—into something else entirely with the addition of a few of them scattered on top. Neutral Pop Rocks (listed as pastry rocks) are available at www.chefrubber.com.

Plum Crostata

Have you sworn you'll never bake a pie? Here's your answer. It's infinitely easier—a single crust, rolled out free-form and folded over glistening fruit—and I think of it as pie's sexier sister.

SERVES 4 TO 6

YOU'LL NEED:
food processor,
parchment
paper

Dough

1 cup (2 sticks) unsalted butter

2⅔ cups all-purpose flour

5 tablespoons confectioners' sugar

½ teaspoon salt

⅔ cup ice water

Filling

½ cup apricot, plum, or peach preserves

6 ripe prune plums (about 1 pound), halved, pitted, and cut in ¼" slices

1 tablespoon unsalted butter, melted

2 tablespoons granulated sugar

CUT THE BUTTER into ½" pieces, place on a plate, and chill in the freezer for 10 minutes.

MEANWHILE, COMBINE the flour, confectioners' sugar, and salt in a food processor. Pulse to blend. Add the butter pieces and pulse 3 or 4 times for about 4 seconds each, just until the mixture looks like very coarse bread crumbs (the butter should be in pea-sized pieces). Add the ice water and pulse for 5 to 10 seconds until the dough *just* comes together. Streaks of pure butter in the dough are okay. Turn the dough out onto a lightly floured board, press into a thick disk, and wrap in plastic. Refrigerate for at least 1 hour or overnight. If chilled for more than 1 hour, let the dough stand for 10 to 30 minutes before rolling out.

PREHEAT THE OVEN to 400°F and place a rack in the center.

PLACE A SHEET of parchment paper on a work surface and dust generously with flour. Place the dough in the center and roll it out into a large rectangle, approximately 15" × 20"; don't worry if the edges are rough and uneven. Slide the parchment onto a baking sheet.

BRUSH THE PRESERVES over the dough, leaving a 2" border. Arrange the plums over the preserves in concentric circles, overlapping the slices slightly. Lift the edges of the dough and fold them in over the plums, pinching the dough into pleats as you fold. Brush the top of the dough with the melted butter and sprinkle the granulated sugar over the whole tart. Bake for about 35 minutes, until the crust is bubbling and browned and the plums are bubbling tender. Slide the tart from the parchment onto a rack and cool for 10 minutes. Serve, cut in wedges, warm or at room temperature.

Cotton Candy

If cotton candy is just for carnivals and street fairs, why is it a fixture at The Four Seasons and other Michelin-starred restaurants like Anthos? Because it's fun, it's beautiful, and it's dead easy to make. As you may have noticed, I'm not big on cooking gadgets, but my mini cotton candy maker was worth every penny. Stick to white sugar and serve it in a white bowl or footed compote. It's my go-to dessert when I don't have time. It's a foolproof crowd-pleaser.

YOU'LL NEED: cotton candy maker	1 tablespoon granulated sugar per person	Multicolored sanding sugar

PLACE THE GRANULATED SUGAR in the cotton candy machine and follow the manufacturer's instructions. Using a wooden spoon, catch the cotton candy as it is made, twirling the spoon as you go. Slide off the spoon onto a footed compote and dust with the sanding sugar.

donatella clicks

You can order Hammacher Schlemmer's Retro Series or Tabletop Cotton Candy Maker at www.shop.com. A huge selection of sanding sugar is available at www.thebakerskitchen.net.

Strawberry Semifreddo

Literally translated, *semifreddo* means "partially frozen." Its texture is achieved by incorporating air into the strawberries and cream mixture. It's simpler to make than ice cream, more intriguing than mousse, yet shares the best qualities of both. The beauty of semifreddo is that you can mold it in just about any container, from wax-coated paper cups (torn away before serving), a loaf pan (for slicing in slabs), or silicone muffin tins (for shaped desserts). If you chill it in a tub, you can scoop it straight from the container.

Tuaca is a golden liqueur made in Tuscany. It infuses the semifreddo with the subtle flavors of orange and vanilla.

SERVES 6 TO 8

YOU'LL NEED:
loaf pan, food processor, electric mixer

---

4 cups strawberries, hulled, plus more for garnish

¼ cup sugar

3 tablespoons Tuaca or Grand Marnier, optional

1 cup heavy cream

Fresh mint, cut in thin strips, for garnish (optional)

LINE AN 8" OR 9" × 5" × 3" LOAF PAN, if using, with plastic wrap and set aside.

COMBINE THE STRAWBERRIES, sugar, and Tuaca in the bowl of a food processor and puree. Reserve 1 cup. Pour the remaining puree into a large bowl. Whip the cream in another bowl using an electric mixer until soft peaks form when you lift the beaters out of the bowl. Fold the cream into the puree using a rubber spatula, working from the bottom of the bowl, until there are no signs of cream. Pour the mixture into the loaf pan, cover with plastic wrap, and freeze until firm, about 2 hours.

INVERT THE SEMIFREDDO onto a serving plate. Remove the plastic wrap and, when slightly softened, smooth the top with a knife. Cut into ¾"- to 1"-thick slices and garnish with the strawberries, mint, and some of the reserved puree drizzled on top.

Rice Pudding

Pastiera, a wheat berry and ricotta pie sweetened with citron and subtly infused with orange flower water, is always served on Easter in Italian homes, especially in Naples, where the tradition began. My father misses this dish more than any other from his childhood. Several years ago, I traveled to Naples to learn how to make the *pastiera* from my second mom, Rita DeRosa. After dozens of attempts to duplicate hers (and just as many thumbs-down from my dad), I finally mastered it. Now he insists I make it at every holiday.

This rice pudding is inspired by that special dessert. I've recast the pie filling and gotten rid of the crust altogether to make this a sure (and delicious) thing on the first try. Italian grocery stores carry jars of cooked wheat berries, which makes preparing it so much easier.

SERVES 6 TO 8

¾ cup dried wheat berries

1 bay leaf

5 cups whole milk

½ cup sugar

¾ cup arborio or Carnaroli rice

1 vanilla bean, split, or ¼ teaspoon pure vanilla extract

1 teaspoon ground cinnamon

¾ cup candied orange peel or citron, finely chopped

2 tablespoons orange blossom water or orange or lemon extract

Candied vanilla bean, for garnish

Strips of candied orange peel, for garnish (optional)

BRING A SAUCEPAN OF WATER to a brisk simmer. Add the wheat berries and the bay leaf and cook until the grains are tender with just a little resistance at the center, about 45 minutes. A few grains will have burst. Drain and set aside.

COMBINE THE MILK, sugar, rice, vanilla bean halves, and cinnamon in a large saucepan. Bring to a boil, then reduce to a simmer and cook, stirring frequently, about 25 minutes, until the mixture is very creamy and the rice is completely tender. Remove from the heat and stir in the vanilla extract, if using. Let stand for 10 minutes. Stir in ½ cup of the orange peel, the wheat berries, and orange blossom water. Garnish with the remaining orange peel and the candied vanilla bean. Serve warm or chilled. The pudding will thicken as it cools.

donatella clicks

Pleasant Hill Grain (www.pleasanthillgrain.com) carries dozens of grains, including wheat berries. For candied orange peel, citron, and vanilla bean as well as orange blossom water, visit The Great American Spice Company (www. americanspice.com). www.apilcina.com has long pretty strips of candied peel.

Pumpkin Bread Pudding

My pastry chef Zak Miller says he prefers pumpkin puree straight from a can to making his own puree. I love hearing this from an established chef—it's like getting permission to skip the hard part. The beautiful thing about bread pudding is that it can't fall like a soufflé or fail to set like a flan. It's very forgiving, which is perfect if you're a baker like me who gets impatient with too much precision! I like to make this with a dense, well-structured bread such as a day-old rustic French or Italian loaf or, at Christmastime, panettone. You can bake it in individual ramekins if you prefer; just reduce the baking time to 40 minutes and place the ramekins on a baking sheet. Be sure to poke the pudding to see if any uncooked custard bubbles up from the bottom before removing it from the oven.

SERVES 8 TO 10

YOU'LL NEED:
loaf pan

---

4 cups whole milk

¼ cup heavy cream

8 large eggs

1 cup granulated sugar

2 teaspoons ground cinnamon

½ teaspoon ground cloves

½ teaspoon ground nutmeg

1 (15-ounce) can pumpkin puree

½ pound bread, sliced thick and torn into large chunks

Butter and brown sugar for preparing the pan

2 cups heavy cream

2 tablespoons confectioners' sugar

COMBINE THE MILK, cream, eggs, sugar, cinnamon, cloves, nutmeg, and pumpkin puree in a large bowl. Whisk until smooth. Add the bread and stir to be sure all the bread is evenly moistened. Cover and let soak at least 4 hours or overnight in the refrigerator.

PREHEAT THE OVEN to 275°F. Grease a 9" × 5" loaf pan with butter and dust with brown sugar.

LADLE THE PUDDING MIXTURE into the loaf pan or ramekins and bake until set, about 1½ hours. Whip the cream and sugar together just until it forms soft mounds. Cut the pudding in slices, top with a dollop of whipped cream, and serve warm.

Roasted Pears with Chocolate Sauce and Amaretti

This is the sweet, seductive, and perfect ending to a meal of filet mignon (page 136). Roasted pears drizzled with chocolate couldn't be more romantic. Amaretti cookies (Di Saronno are my favorite), crumbled and strewn on top, make the perfect flavor and texture pairing. To ripen hard pears, place them in a paper bag until the stem end gives a little. This does not happen overnight—it can take a few days—so plan accordingly. You can drizzle with a little Easy Chocolate Sauce, too, if you want to gild the lily.

SERVES 4 TO 6

2 tablespoons fresh lemon juice

4–6 ripe Bosc pears

½ cup light brown sugar, packed

2 tablespoons unsalted butter

2 tablespoons cider

1 cinnamon stick

1 star anise

3 whole cloves

Grated zest of 1 orange

12–18 amaretti cookies, crumbled

PREHEAT THE OVEN to 350°F.

FILL A LARGE BOWL with water and add the lemon juice. Peel the pears and cut them in half lengthwise, leaving the stem intact. Slide into the acidulated water to prevent them from turning brown. When all of the pears are peeled, remove them from the water, pat dry and place in a shallow baking dish with the brown sugar, butter, cider, cinnamon stick, star anise, cloves, and orange zest. Bake, basting every 15 minutes, until the pears are tender, about 45 minutes. Arrange 2 pear halves on each dessert plate, drizzle with the chocolate sauce, and top with the crumbled amaretti.

donatella clicks

The iconic red tins of Lazzaroni Amaretti di Saronno are ubiquitous in gourmet food shops, but if you can't find them, you will online at www.amazon.com.

Easy Chocolate Sauce

MAKES 2 CUPS

4 ounces dark bittersweet chocolate, preferably Valrhona, coarsely chopped

1 cup unsweetened cocoa powder

¾ cup sugar

1¼ cups heavy cream

Pinch of salt

COMBINE THE CHOCOLATE and cocoa powder in a medium bowl and set aside. Combine the sugar, cream, salt, and ½ cup water in a saucepan and bring to a low boil. Pour the hot liquid over the chocolate and whisk until smooth. Keep warm until ready to serve.

My favorite party trick

Several years ago, I was out with friends at a resort in Puglia. We were on a balcony nibbling on amaretti cookies when the host, in a scene straight out of *Big Night*, took us by surprise by lighting her cookie wrapper with a match. The paper burned uneventfully for a few seconds, and then shot up to the sky like a firefly and flamed out. It was magical and a little romantic.

The cookies themselves have a poignant back story. To celebrate the arrival of the Cardinal of Milan to the town of Saronno, a local newlywed couple whipped up these airy, bittersweet cookies and wrapped them in pairs to symbolize their love.

Ice Wine Jell-O Shots

Humor can be a host's most attractive asset—if you're not having fun, your guests won't either. This elegant riff on the college party "cocktail" does not involve knocking anything back in a sudden move. It's flavored with ice wine, a sweet dessert wine that is produced from grapes that have been frozen on the vine. These intriguing "shots" are meant to be eaten gracefully with a spoon. Inniskillin is considered the Rolls-Royce of ice wine; save it for drinking and choose a less pricey bottle for the Jell-O shots. An open bottle of ice wine will last 3 to 5 days. Frozen grapes are as easy as can be, but most people like them slushy rather than hard as ice, so don't leave them in the freezer for more than 35 to 40 minutes.

SERVES 4 TO 6

YOU'LL NEED: parchment paper, shot glasses

---

2 teaspoons powdered unflavored gelatin

1 (375-milliliter) bottle ice wine

Seedless red and green grapes, for serving

SPRINKLE THE GELATIN over 2 tablespoons of cold water in a small saucepan. Soak for about 5 minutes, until softened. Add 2 tablespoons of ice wine to the gelatin mixture and warm the mixture over low heat, just until the gelatin melts and the mixture is completely smooth. Remove from the heat and transfer to a metal bowl. Add the remaining wine. Cool to room temperature, then ladle into 4 or 6 small glasses. Chill until set, about 2 hours. Alternatively, pour the mixture into a shallow square pan. Chill until set, then cut into 1" cubes.

ABOUT 30 MINUTES before serving, rinse the grapes with cold water and spread them on a parchment-lined baking sheet without touching one another. Place in the freezer until serving time. Arrange the ice wine shots on a platter and surround with the partially frozen grapes.

ACKNOWLEDGMENTS

There are many people to whom I owe my gratitude:

First and foremost, my parents. They shaped who I have become and have always made it clear that family (and food) is the most important thing in the world. My father, a renowned restaurateur himself, taught me the business. Eating my mother's cooking every night of my childhood—and spending summers with my aunts in Puglia and Naples—left an indelible imprint on my cooking style. Kathleen Hackett put my voice on paper. Thank you for your patience and for your ability to make me laugh. My editor, Pam Krauss, believed in me and is just hands-down the best there is. Thanks also to Michael Psaltis, my book agent, for always protecting me. To my angels on set: Anna Williams, for her kindness, her eye, and her stunning photography; Philippa Brathwaite, for her joy and brilliant prop styling; and Jee Levine, an artist and a perfectionist, who made every crumb perfect. You all made my vision come alive exactly as I wanted!

Davide Torchio, my hair magician, and partner Fabrice Borg always make me look my best. Thanks for being such wonderful friends. My friends and neighbors, renowned interior designer David Scott and Stefano Antoniazzi opened their stunning home and allowed me to shoot the party scenes there. My executive assistant, Matthew Pober, was the angel I needed; thank you for your dedication. To my support team in all my restaurants, especially Matthew Gardiner, my talented and dedicated Director of Operations; thank you for always having my back and for being such a loyal friend. Ron Brannon believed in me before anyone else did and always encouraged me to become all that I could be; thank you for standing by me all these

My angels, Giancarlo, Francesco, and Elisa

years. I must also thank Fran Renda for giving me wings to fly. To my namesake, Aunt Donata, an incredible cook who has always been there for me. Many thanks to Maurizio Derosa for always challenging me with his vast knowledge of wine and food, and to his Neapolitan mother, Rita Derosa, for teaching me many of her culinary secrets!

To my big brother and sister, Umberto and Annamaria, for your unconditional love, support, and laughter through the years. To my brother-in-law Frank and my sister-in-law Marta, thanks for always being my biggest fans! Finally, to my five beautiful nieces and nephews, Giancarlo, Francesco, Elisa, Sofia, and Olivia, you are the joys of my life!

Credits

My book would not have come to life so beautifully without the gorgeous props provided by the following:

Barneys New York, Bergdorf Goodman, Brilliant Surface, Caleb Siemon, Calvin Klein Home, Chilewich, The Conran Shop, Crate & Barrel, Dean & Deluca, Heather Palmer Glass, Joe Cariati, Juliska, Keena, Kiln Design Studio, Magasin Totale, Michael Wainwright, Nicole Farhi, and Sur La Table

INDEX